WISDOM OF THE EAST

BRAHMA KNOWLEDGE

WISDOM OF THE EAST

BRAHMA KNOWLEDGE

AN OUTLINE OF THE PHILOSOPHY OF THE VEDANTA AS SET FORTH BY THE UPANISHADS AND BY SANKARA

BY

L. D. BARNETT, M.A., Litt. D.

PROFESSOR OF SANSKRIT AT UNIVERSITY COLLEGE, LONDON

GYAN

Published by

GYAN

Gyan Publishing House
5, Ansari Road
Daryaganj, New Delhi-110002
Phone: 011-47034999, 9811692060
E-mail: books@gyanbooks.com

Distribution Network
gyanbooks.com
India, USA, Canada, UK, Australia, France

ISBN : 978-81-212-2186-3 (HB)
First Published, 1907

2nd Impression 2021

Printed at: Gyan Press, Delhi.

Wisdom of the East, Brahma Knowledge
Author: L. D. Barnett

WISDOM OF THE EAST

BRAHMA-KNOWLEDGE

AN OUTLINE OF THE PHILOSOPHY OF THE VEDĀNTA AS SET FORTH BY THE UPANISHADS AND BY ŚANKARA

BY L D BARNETT, M A, LITT D
PROFESSOR OF SANSKRIT AT UNIVERSITY COLLEGE, LONDON

LONDON
JOHN MURRAY, ALBEMARLE STREET
1907

CONTENTS

PART II

SOME TEXTS OF THE VEDĀNTA

EDITORIAL NOTE

EDITORIAL NOTE

THE object of the Editors of this series is a very definite one They desire above all things that, in their humble way, these books shall be the ambassadors of good-will and understanding between East and West—the old world of Thought and the new of Action In this endeavour, and in their own sphere, they are but followers of the highest example in the land They are confident that a deeper knowledge of the great ideals and lofty philosophy of Oriental thought may help to a revival of that true spirit of Charity which neither despises nor fears the nations of another creed and colour Finally, in thanking press and public for the very cordial reception given to the "Wisdom of the East" series, they wish to state that no pains have been spared to secure the best specialists for the treatment of the various subjects at hand

L CRANMER-BYNG
S A KAPADIA

NORTHBROOK SOCIETY,
185 PICCADILLY, W

INTRODUCTION

THE following pages sketch in outline—and therefore inadequately—the most important elements in the series of ideas which, under the general name of *Vedānta*, have been in one form or another the basis of all Indian thought worthy of the name No attempt is made here either to justify or to refute them Their philosophic weakness is obvious no less patent is the intensity of the longing for an intellectual resting-place, a "Rock of Ages," which has driven millions of the most thoughtful Hindus to drown their soul's disquiet in the utterly blank abstraction of "Brahma"

In the main the Vedānta agrees with the teaching of Parmenides and the early Eleatics of his school, and has many points of contact with Plato's idealism But whereas the Greek philosophers were only professors, the Vedānta has always had a deep practical significance Like the early Christian Church it preached as highest consummation the renunciation of the world and of self, passing in some of its phases into a religious self-surrender fully equal in completeness, if not superior, to that of European monasticism, and even as a purely intellectual force it has had an incalculable influence upon the minds and characters of millions of Hindus in nearly every station of civilised life To discuss this issue is beyond the province of our book, it must suffice to point to it

PART I

AN ACCOUNT OF THE VEDĀNTA

§ 1 VEDĀNTA, THE VEDAS' END —The Sanskrit word *Vedānta* (*veda-anta*) signifies "end" or "bound of the Vedas" It was originally given, at a somewhat advanced stage of their development, to the works called *Upanishads*, and subsequently to the various philosophies claiming to be based upon them Besides the Upanishads, one of these philosophies will be noticed in the following pages, namely the system promulgated in the ninth century by Śankara in his great commentary (*Śārīraka-bhāshya*) upon the epitome of Upanishadic doctrine commonly known as the *Brahma-sūtra*, or "Aphorisms of Brahma," and traditionally ascribed to one or the other of the legendary sages Bādarāyana and Vyāsa

§ 2 THE FOUR VEDAS —The hymns of the *Ṛig-veda*, composed by various authors some three thousand years ago, are almost the only monument of the first period of Indian thought, for the collections known as the *Yajur-veda* and

Sāma-veda are for the most part merely adaptations of the Rig-veda for special liturgical purposes, while the *Atharva-veda*, which was not admitted until much later into the Vedic canon, combines Rig-vedic hymns selected for ritual objects with a mass of various incantations of little or no philosophic and literary merit The study of these hymn-collections in their liturgical application by the Brahman schools bore as fruit the bulky volumes known generically as *Brāhmanas*

§ 3 THE UPANISHADS [1]—The earlier Upanishads, a series of philosophic tracts of varying length and character, arose in the schools of the Brāhmanas, and especially were attached to the sections of the latter styled *Āranyakas* The Hindus class together Vedas, Brāhmanas, Āranyakas, and Upanishads under the general title of "Veda" (knowledge) or "Revelation" (*śruti*, "hearing")

The Vedas and Brāhmanas are the handbooks of a crude naturalistic ritualism, but the Āranyakas ("Forest-books"), apparently intended

[1] The etymology of the word *Upanishad* is not clear European scholars generally regard it as from the root *sad* (compare Latin *sedeo*), so that it would mean "a sitting before," i e a lesson, but native tradition interprets it as "mystery," and the enigmatic formulae in which the older Upanishads sometimes convey their theories lend some support to this view (see Deussen, *Philosophy of Upanishads*, English translation, pp 10 ff)

for the study of anchorites in the woods, where the more elaborate liturgies were suspended, deal more with the theory of ritual, chiefly from an allegorical point of view Hence they lead over to the earlier Upanishads, which express a series of generally cognate metaphysical and psychological ideas, at first by allegorical interpretation of Vedic ritual and myth, later with increasing independence of method Their relation towards Vedic ritualism was at first one of opposition, preaching the saving grace of knowledge alone, they regarded as inadequate the actual liturgies, which admittedly aimed only at worldly welfare Later their attitude became more conciliatory, and we find them styling themselves *Vedānta* (first Mund III II 6, Śvet VI 22)

§ 4 FOUNDATIONS OF UPANISHADIC IDEAS — The Rig-veda contains many strata of religious and philosophic thought Its oldest element is a worship of nature-deities, such as the Sky-Father, Earth-Mother, Dawn, etc, who were inherited from the time before the division of the Indo-European stocks These figures, however, are not as a rule living forces in religion, for the most part they are kept alive merely by conservatism and poetic convention The most real gods of the Vedic pantheon are peculiarly Indian Often indeed a distant connection can be traced between them and nature-deities in the other Indo-European races, but their myths and legends have undergone a long process of development on Indian soil, by which they have acquired the characteristic stamp of the Hindu genius But even in the naturalistic polytheism of this mythology we can trace in the Rig-veda, especially in its later parts, a tendency towards a pantheism merging all being into a Supreme Spirit of vaguely defined character, a primal Infinite

Thus "there is one Existence, sages call it by many names" (Rig-veda, i clxiv 46, cf x cxiv 5) The primitive spirit and source of being is called *Hiranya-garbha* ("Germ of Gold"), or Prajā-pati ("Lord of Creatures"), x cxxi, as his own firstborn he enters the universe created by him (x lxxii, lxxxii, etc) In x cxxix the first Being is neither existent nor non-existent, a watery void, from which arose a primal Unity, whence sprang Desire as first bond between being and non-being Another poet (x xc) tells how the universe arose from *Purusha*, "Man," that is, an ideal human sacrifice offered by the gods For as, to the Vedic mind, a sacrifice is a power controlling Nature, and the human sacrifice is the most powerful of all, then the greatest of all forces, the cosmogonic energies, must have arisen from an ideal offering of this kind made by the highest agents, the gods

To the demand of philosophy for a final and absolute Reality beyond the temporary and merely relative reality of phenomenal experience the Vedic poets thus gave almost the same answer as the early Greek thinkers They asserted, in very diverse and often very mystic terms, the existence of a single cosmic matter or World-Spirit, whom they styled variously *Prajā-pati*, *Brahmā* (masculine), *Purusha*, *Hiranya-garbha*, etc

§ 5 BRAHMA AND PRĀNA —This conception, however it might be disguised in cosmogonic and mythopoeic forms, was in essence strictly materialistic But by its side there arose in the schools of the Brāhmanas two somewhat different currents of thought—the doctrines of *Brahma* and of *Prāna* *Brahma*, in the earlier Vedic books, is a neuter noun, meaning the spell or prayer of the priest and the magic power which it exerts over gods, men, and the universe *Prāṇa*, again, is properly the breath of the body, hence the incorporeal forces or functional energies on which depends the existence of material life Thus arose the idea of Force, cosmic power, *Brahma*, as the ultimate reality and origin of phenomenal being, the knowledge of which brought with it the knowledge of all the phenomena evolved from it

Often the Upanishads, especially the older texts, identify Brahma (and the individual Self which is one with Brahma), with the "life-breath" in the microcosm and its analogue, the wind of the macrocosm On the supremacy of the breath over the other functions, see B A I v 14, Ch I xi 5, V i 6 f , VI vii , VII xv , Pra VI 3 f , breath or wind the guiding force of nature, B A I v 21 f , III iii 2, vii 2 f , first principle of nature, Kau II 12 f

In the same mythological fashion Brahma is often symbolised by the *manas*, or organ of determinate sense-perception and will (see § 18), and by the ether, the macrocosmic analogue of the *manas*

The earlier Upanishads often also speak of the cosmic principle as *Purusha*, literally "man" This term, as we have seen, arises from the Vedic hymn which mystically describes the origin of the world from the body of an ideal man sacrificed by the gods , hence it often denotes the Demiurge, or first principle of cosmic life (with a false etymology from *puri-śaya*, "lying in the city," viz in the microcosmic and macrocosmic body), and sometimes is used loosely for spirit generally

As the sun is sometimes mentioned as a symbol of Brahma, so also Brahma is sometimes typified macrocosmically by the *purusha* in the sun and microcosmically by the *purusha* in the eye (i e the reflected figure in the pupil)

Another symbol of Brahma as identified with the individual soul is the bodily heat (Ch III. xiii 7 f) In Ch IV x-xv the sacred fires are identified with Brahma, to which are given the especial attributes of space (*kham*) and joy (*kam*) See further §§ 8, 22

§ 6 DOCTRINE OF TRANSMIGRATION AND WORKS —At this point we may note two new ideas which henceforth dominated Indian thought—transmigration of the soul (*samsāra*, literally "wandering") and the influence of works (*karma*) The Vedic Hindu was passionately convinced of the joy of life, the Hindu of a later generation no less impressed by its misery This pessimism finds expression in two ideas The first is that the only life worth living is that vouchsafed to the few elect—union of the soul with the transcendent Brahma, all other existence, whatever it may seem, is wretched, an infinite number of souls flitting in constant sorrow and blindness through every degree of organic embodiment The second idea is that every instant of experience is the rigidly predetermined resultant of a previous act, a present pleasure is the requital of a relatively good deed, a present sorrow the repayment of an ill deed, in a previous life, and every act whatsoever, whether of deed, thought, or speech, is absolutely evil, as attaching the soul still further to the fetters of embodiment Gloomy and impracticable as is this attitude, it is simply a phase of extreme idealism

§ 7 ĀTMĀ, SELF OR SPIRIT —The word *ātmā* is several times used in the Rig-veda with the meaning of "breath," "spirit," in the literal sense, and so far there was little to distinguish it from the word *prāna* (§ 5) But from this sense was further evolved the meaning "self" Then we can imagine that men began to reflect upon their own words What, they doubtless asked, is the "self" of which we speak when we use sentences like "he finds it out by [him]self," "he goes by [him]self," "he sees [him]self"? It must be the inmost essence, the indwelling reality, the *αὐτό* of each agent, the informing *εἶδος* of subjecthood Therefore it must be thought itself For subjecthood is a mode of thought, and to thought or will all action is finally traceable And the *Ātmā*, the Self, the consciousness of self-identity on which is based all further ideation of the thinking subject, is one with *Brahma*, the universal Power My Idea is the World-Idea, "I am Brahma"

There is another link in this chain The Vedic poets speak now and then of a god *Daksha*, who, as his name implies, is simply the abstract idea of "skill" or "intelligence" rather vaguely personified, and twice (x v 7, lxxii 4, 5) Daksha is regarded as primal Being and universal father, from whom sprang the great gods and the universe Thus Vedic mythology furnished two fruitful ideas—that the objective universe sprang from Intelligence, *Daksha*, and from an ideal Man, *Purusha*, and hence grew up gradually the idealistic conception of the universe as arising from, and existing in, the Thought of man

§ 8 UPANISHADIC PRINCIPLES —These conceptions, which are conveyed by the Upanishads in very diverse and often mystic and contradictory utterances, may be summed up in three propositions Firstly, the whole of finite or phenomenal being is evolved from an infinite and unconditioned substrate of absolute reality, *Brahma* Secondly, Brahma is pure Thought, absolute Spirit Thirdly, Brahma is one with the essential thought of each individual subject of thought, the Soul or *Ātmā*

Sankara, in following these principles, lays down a broad distinction between Brahma as absolute, unqualified, and indeterminate (*nirguna*), and Brahma as secondary, determined by self-imposed limitations of space, time, and causality (*saguna*) The former is real, and object of real knowledge , the latter is essentially unreal, an illusion arising from the congenital error of the subject of thought, and vanishing away as soon as the latter by enlightenment ceases to conceive the Absolute in forms of determinate thought, and realises his essential unity with it Thus all objects of thought must be regarded from two standpoints the first is that of empiric experience, determined by conditions of space, time, and causality , the second is transcendental, admitting the existence of nothing but an absolute unqualified One Sankara argues from both standpoints without much regard for consistency He justifies the Upanishadic habit of describing Brahma under the qualified forms of empirical thought, or as represented by a symbol, as a concession to feebler intellects, which cannot comprehend an abstract and unqualified principle, and are by these representations induced to worship Brahma in his qualified character, and thereby to attain freedom from ignorance and sin, worldly welfare, and "gradual release," *krama-mukti* (see § 25), whereas the true essence of Brahma is conveyed only by those passages which deny of him all qualification (see especially his commentary on Ch VIII I and on Brahma-sūtra, I III 14 f, III II 11 f)

§ 9 ORIGIN OF UNIVERSE FROM BRAHMA — I *Upanishads* —The Upanishads, being the work of Brahmans, are naturally influenced to a great extent by the naturalism of Vedic myth, especially in their conception of the origination of the universe from Brahma As we saw (§ 4), the Veda already speaks of a primal Being that created a phenomenal world from itself and became its indwelling soul, and thus, by its empiric distinction between the first Being as cause and the world as its effect, the Veda has arrived at a pantheistic standpoint

From this the Upanishadic authors started, and struggled slowly towards the strictly idealistic position from which the universe, organic and inorganic, subjects and objects, is regarded as a single Idea which is the same as the Idea of the individual subject of thought In this progress they still made frequent use of the Vedic ideas and the mythical forms embodying them, they admitted their distinction of Brahma as cause and the world as effect, but admitted it as a mode of empiric thought of merely relative validity, while from the standpoint of transcendental reality they asserted the identity of the two

Brahma (Ātmā), causing the hitherto unconditioned universe to become conditioned as Name and Form (the elements of cogitable being), entered into it "up to the nail-tips" as immanent soul, B A I iv 7, cf Ch VI ii 3, iii 3, Ait I i 11 f, Taitt II 6 Brahma is wholly present as its soul in every living thing, B A II i 16, iv, III iv, v, Ch VI viii-xvi The Cosmic Soul, Hiranya-garbha or Brahmā (masculine), enters into creation as first-born of Brahma (neuter), or highest manifestation, B A II v ("the brilliant immortal Male," *Purusha*), Ait III iii (Brahma-Ātmā is intelligence), Kau I Brahma is Cosmic Soul, universal subject of thought from which arise the principles of finite thought (*mahān ātmā*, Kath III 10, *mahān purushah*, Svet III 19) The world is created from and by Brahma as the web from the spider, sparks from fire, B A II i 20, Svet VI 10, Mund I i 7, II i 1 Brahma is "the Eternal cloaked by (empirical) reality," B A I vi 3, cf I iv 7, II iv 12, v 18, etc, Ch. III xiv. 1, IV. iv-ix, VI xiii, etc The individual soul, according to the Upanishads, does not exist previous to the creation by Brahma

The universe is created from water, B A I v 13, Ch VII x 1, Ait I 1 Three elements, B A I ii 2, Ch VI ii (heat, water, and food, successively created one from the other, after which each was blended with part of the others) Five elements (adding ether and wind), Taitt II i., Pra IV 8

II *Later Vedānta* —Śankara (on Brahma-sūtra, II iii 1 f) endeavours to reconcile the discrepant cosmogonic theories of Ch VI ii and Taitt II i, by laying down that from the Self arises ether, thence wind, thence fire, thence water, thence earth, and that this process is reversed on the dissolution of the universe With this qualification he follows the Ch in its derivation of inorganic nature from heat (fire), water, and food (earth) These he regards as primitive subtle elements, which by being mixed together form the gross elements, a gross element is produced by the predominance of the corresponding subtle element in admixture with the other two For his metaphysical explanation of creation, see § 12

Śankara does not mention the theory of quintuplication (*panchīkarana*) adopted by the later Vedānta This doctrine assumes that there are five elements—ether, air, fire, water, earth—in both subtle and gross forms, in order that a particular gross element, e g water, may arise, it is necessary that a proportion of one-half of the corresponding subtle form of water be mixed with a proportion of one-half of the half of the other four subtle elements These five elements, according to the same theory, arise from the union of the Cosmic Self or *Īśvara* with cosmic ignorance, in the order above mentioned (see further below, § 12)

§ 10 BRAHMA IS ABSOLUTE BEING —The question whether the universal substrate, or Brahma, should properly be called being (*sat*) or non-being (*a-sat*), already agitated the Vedic poets (see Rig-veda, X cxxix 1), and passed through the schools of the Brāhmanas to those of the older Upanishads The debate, however, was merely over words As Brahma is beyond all the limiting conditions of phenomenal being, either term may be applied to it, it is at once metaphysically existent and empirically non-existent

Brahma is *non-being*, B A II iii 1, Ch III xix 1, Taitt II vi-vii , *being*, Ch VI ii 1, etc Brahma is "reality of reality,' B A II i 20, iii 6, "the Eternal cloaked in (empirical) reality," I vi 3 A reconciliation from the transcendental standpoint is found in Śvet IV 18, V 1, Mund II ii 1, etc Śankara (on Brahma-sūtra, I iv 14 f) rightly notes the twofold meaning of the terms "being" and "not-being"

§ 11 BRAHMA IS THOUGHT —The Vedic *brahma*, "prayer" or "spell," is naturally a function of intellect, and when it had risen to the rank of a cosmic Force, it retained this character It is the universal subject of thought, but as it is itself the universe, and there is nothing beside, it is also its own object, like the Aristotelian νόησις νοήσεως, and as it is above the conditions of space, time, and causality, we can say of it only that it *exists*, and is *Thought*

Frequently, from the natural tendency to conceive a higher sphere of existence as a realm of light and thought as itself light, Brahma and the individual Self identified with it are described as supreme self-luminous light B A IV IV 16, Ch VIII III 4, XII 3, Kath V 15, Śvet VI 14

§ 12 BRAHMA IS ĀTMĀ—I *Upanishads*—This idealistic conception became more marked when Brahma was identified with the *Ātmā*, the subject of individual thought "The universe is an Idea, *my* Idea"—this doctrine is constantly preached in detailed expositions and in pithy phrases like the famous "I am Brahma" (*aham brahmāsmi*), "thou art that" (*tat tvam asi*) Hence all phenomena are known when their substrate Brahma is known as the Self of the knower

For *tat tvam asi* see Ch VI VIII 7 f, *aham brahmāsmi*, B A I IV. 10, cf *tad vai tat*, "truly this is that," B A V IV, *etad vai tat*, Kath IV 3–6 The most adequate treatment of this theme is B A IV III–IV the Self is "the Spirit (*Purusha*)

made of understanding amid the Breaths, the inward light within the heart, that travels abroad, remaining the same, through both worlds," wandering in waking and dreaming through this world, and in deep sleep or death through the world of Brahma, in dreams it builds up a fairy world from the materials of waking thought, in dreamless sleep it is merged in the "understanding self," *prājna ātmā*, viz Brahma as universal subject of thought, without consciousness of objects distinct from itself (cf §§ 11, 15, 18) Ātmā is pure consciousness, Kau III f, as a purely intellectual force pervading all being, it is compared to salt dissolved in water, B A II IV 12, Ch VI XIII Ātmā known, all is known, Ch VI I f, the later view of it as impassive spectator of the subjects, objects, and activity of finite thought, Pra VI 5, Śvet VI 11, Sarvopanishat-sāra, etc

Ch VIII I f lays special emphasis on the presence of the whole macrocosm, the universal Self, in the heart of man, and hence on the absolute freedom of him who knows the Self within him. The whole world of cognitions exists for us only in so far as it enters into the range of our egoity; our pleasures are only for the satisfaction of our Self, which is the All, this recognition unites our soul with the universe and gives us control of all things from their source, B A II IV, IV V The final reality of cognition is infinitude, *bhūmā*, illimitable ideation, on realising which the soul wins absolute freedom, Ch VII xxiii f

Very important in this connection is the theory of the Five Selves propounded in the Taittirīya Upanishad, ii , an attempt to interpret the phenomena of physical existence in terms of the Ātmā The author conceives the first four Selves as sheaths surrounding the fifth The first is *anna-maya*, " formed of food ", that is, it comprises the physical organs of microcosmic and macrocosmic body Within this is the second, the *prāna-maya*, " formed of life-breaths ", it is the Self as embodied in the incorporeal functions on which depends the activity of the gross organs in the microcosm and macrocosm The third is *mano-maya*, " formed of will," namely of the Vedas and Brāhmanas, which are the powers inspiring the life of the world for worldly ends, for they ordain rituals for the carnal benefit of gods and their worshippers in this and other worlds The fourth is *vijnāna-maya*, " formed of understanding," namely that phase of consciousness in which the vanity of this Vedic ritual is recognised and superseded by an intellectual worship of Brahma, which however still distinguishes Brahma as object from the Self as worshipper Within this is the inmost Self, the *ānanda-maya*, " formed of bliss," the incogitable spirit of infinite peace and joy (cf Ch IV x-xv, where Brahma is essentially space and joy)

II *Later Vedānta*—The triad of attributes often mentioned in the later Vedānta, Existence Thought, and Bliss (*sach-chid-ānanda*), does not occur as a formula in Sankara's writings, it is however anticipated by his definition of Brahma as "eternal, omniscient, omnipresent, eternally satisfied, eternally pure, intelligent, and free of nature, understanding, and bliss" (on Brahma-sūtra I 1 4) Brahma is the omnipotent and omniscient cause of the origin, maintenance, and dissolution of the universe, the intelligence forming the Self or true Ego of every being, of which the only possible predicates are absolute Being and Thought (on I 1 2, 4, II III 7, III. II 21, etc)

In accordance with his principles, Sankara regards the creation by and from Brahma from both an esoteric and an exoteric standpoint On the one hand, he remarks, the creation of the phenomenal world as described in terms of empiric thought by the Vedas and Upanishads has no absolute reality at all, it is intended to teach parabolically that the Self of all things is Brahma (see commentary on Brahma-sūtra II I 33) On the other hand, the world of experience cannot be ignored altogether, it is a fact of consciousness, though only of unenlightened consciousness, and accordingly an explanation of its process must be found Creation consists in a division of Brahma by himself into a boundless variety of "names and forms," intelligible existences which constitute the empiric world and possess determinate principles of being, formal and material potentialities (*śakti*) that never vary throughout all the world's successive cycles (see § 23) These potential forces, which relatively to one another are of infinite variety but intrinsically are strictly determinate, include not only the germinal principles of all phenomena but also the empiric souls (*jīva*) as such, and collectively they constitute the "powers" or *śaktis*, i e the eternal demiurgic potencies of Brahma, which in the intervals between the creations of the worlds lie dormant in a deep sleep of illusion as a sum of merely potential energies, waiting for the next creation to arise in cosmopoeic activity (on I iii 30, iv 9, ii i 30 f, etc) Thus the Upanishadic theory of a single creation is replaced by a doctrine of beginningless and endless successions of emergence and reabsorption of the phenomenal world (see § 23)

The force that moves the absolute Idea to conceive itself as a plurality of determinate subjects and objects of empiric thought is, according to Śankara, *Ignorance*, which, though itself strictly negative, is the basis of that positive illusion, the phenomenal world (see § 16) Ignorance creates "determinations," *upādhi*, modes of thought limiting the self-conception of the absolute Brahma, and Ignorance causes the empiric soul thus produced to confuse Brahma with the determinations falsely imposed upon him, so that Brahma is imagined variously as individual soul, a world of experience, and a personal God

The "determinations" that play the most important part in Śankara's system are those which form the structure of individual consciousness by constituting the idea of an embodied individual soul, *jīva* These are the *prānas*, or "breaths," the "works," the "subtle body," the gross body, and sometimes also the sensations and phenomenal perceptions (see § 18) A favourite metaphor by which Śankara illustrates his theory of *upādhis* is that of a jar The space enclosed within a certain jar is really the same as the infinite space filling the universe, and the conception of it as limited by the jar nowise limits the infinitude of space itself, and so the conception of the Self as determined by the forms of embodied existence nowise excludes the identity of the embodied Self with the absolute Brahma The soul itself, says Śankara (on II iii 40), is totally incapable of (empiric) action, whether as subject or object, its apparent activity, e g in desire, grief, etc, is based merely upon Ignorance, for the activity arises because the soul falsely ascribes to itself the properties of "determinations" (cf the definitions of the individual soul given on IV ii 4 as "the intelligent self, *vijnānātmā*, having the determinations of ignorance, works, and previous experience")

The Vedantic schools which followed Śankara

theorised more schematically on the origin of the phenomenal world. They regard Ignorance as a cosmic sum of forces including all finite powers, causes, and effects, which has two characteristic properties, viz. "obscuration" (*āvarana*), causing the Absolute Idea to conceive itself as distinct individual egos, and "distention" (*vikshepa*), arousing in the Self the illusive idea of an external world of phenomena. Accepting the Sānkhya's division of matter into the three *gunas* or modes of *sattva* ("goodness" or "truth"), *rajas* ("passion"), and *tamas* ("gloom"), they identify matter with Cosmic Ignorance, or the sum of individual Ignorances, which acts as a "determinant" to the Supreme Self or Absolute Thought. The latter as "determined" in Cosmic Ignorance acts as a world-soul, directing the universal order of phenomena with supreme power and knowledge, and hence is called *Īśvara*, "the Lord." The Cosmic Ignorance is hence called "Īśvara's body," and also "Deep Sleep" (*sushupti*), for in it the force of Ignorance investing Thought is almost wholly inoperative, and the phenomenal world exists only in potentiality. This sphere of being is called the "sheath of Bliss," *ānandamaya kośa*. To it corresponds a stage of existence in the individual soul, in which the Self or Thought (here styled *Prājna*) is "determined" by individual Ignorance. From Īśvara as "determined" by Cosmic Ignorance arise the subtle elements (§ 18) and thence both the "subtle bodies" (§ 19) and gross elements The "subtle bodies" in the aggregate determine the Self into a mode called *Prāna*, *Sūtrātmā*, or *Hiranya-garbha*, individually they determine it into the mode called *Taijasa* These combinations of matter with the Self form three successive phases of being for the individual soul (1) the "sheath of understanding," *vijnāna-maya kośa*, composed of intelligence (*buddhi*) and the "organs of knowledge" (§ 18), which constitutes the real *agent* in empiric experience, (2) the "sheath of mind," *mano-maya kośa*, formed of *manas* and the organs of action, thus constituting the *instrument* of empiric experience, and (3) the "sheath of the breaths," *prāna-maya kośa*, formed of vital breaths and organs of action, and constituting the *effect* of experience These three phases of being are together called "Dream-Sleep," as in them arise the subtle or elementary forms of phenomena and the reflection of them upon the "determined" Self The gross elements which arise from the subtle collectively "determine" the Self into the phase called *Vaiśvānara* or *Virāt*, individually they "determine" it into *Viśva* This lowest determination is called *anna-maya kośa*, the "sheath of food," or the state of Waking, for into it the forms of both gross and subtle phenomena are displayed to the Self, as in waking both memory and sense-perception are active

The scheme is thus as follows

1 Individual Gross Body, determinant of Viśva, in state of Waking	Sheath of Food	Cosmic Gross Body determinant of Virāt, in state of Waking
2 Individual Subtle Body, determinant of Taijasa, in state of Dreaming	(1) Sheath of Breaths (2) Sheath of Mind (3) Sheath of Understanding	Cosmic Subtle Body, determinant of Prāna, in state of Dreaming
3 Individual Causal Body, determinant of Prājna, in state of Dreamless Sleep	Sheath of Bliss	Cosmic Causal Body, determinant of Īśvara, in state of Dreamless Sleep

§ 13 BRAHMA IS INCOGITABLE —Brahma or Ātmā, being an absolute Reality, the supreme Thing-in-Itself, is therefore inconceivable by the reason, and only capable of being comprehended by an inspired intuition The Self, whether universal or individual, is a single subject of thought, and so cannot be an object of thought, and it is by nature absolute, above all conditions of finite determination This negative conception is most forcibly expressed by the famous formula ascribed to Yājnavalkya, *neti neti*, "not so, not so," a denial of all possible predicates to the Self (B A iv ii 4, iv 22, v 15, etc), and also by frequently describing Brahma or Ātmā in contradictory terms as limitless, infinitely extended and yet immeasurably limited in space and time, and denying to it all activity as cause or effect See also B A ii iv 14, iii iv 2, vii 23, viii 11, Ch iii xiv 2, vii xxiv 1, Kena iii , xi , Kath vi 12 f Sankara (on Brahma-sūtra ii iii 29) explains these contradictions in the description of the size of the Self by asserting that the mention of it as immeasurably small refers to its condition as empiric soul, when it is limited by "determinations" (§ 12) and is conceived under the attributes of the "determination" of intelligence, *buddhi* (§ 18)

Sankara (on Brahma-sūtra iii ii 17) tells a tale of a sage who, on being asked to teach the doctrine of Brahma, remained silent, and on the request being thrice repeated said simply, "I have told you, but you understand not, this Self is still" (cf Ch III xiv 1)

§ 14 PARMENIDES —The opportunity here presents itself to point to the singularly close parallel between Upanishadic thought and the doctrines of the early Eleatic philosophers, and especially Parmenides, who may well have been contemporary with the authors of some of the most important Upanishads Following Xenophanes, who had defined God as eternal, one, and neither in motion nor immobile, Parmenides asserts a single universal Being which is identical with thought Existence is a whole indivisible in space and time, non-being does not exist "Thus there remains but one way to tell of, namely that Being *is* There are many tokens to show that it is unborn and imperishable, whole, only-begotten, unshakeable, and endless Never *was* it nor *will* it be, for it exists entirely in present time, one and indivisible Thus it must exist either absolutely or not at all The power of belief can never admit that from non-being anything else (but non-being) could arise And it (viz, being) is not divisible, for it is identical throughout, nor is there any higher (being) that could prevent its uniformity, nor any less, it is entirely full of being So it is wholly uniform, for being unites with being But it is immobile in the limitations of mighty bonds, beginningless and endless, for birth and destruction have been driven very far away, right conviction has rejected them It abides the same in the same and by itself, and thus remains constantly in its place Thought and the object of thought are the same, for you cannot find thought without the existent thing in which it is expressed There is and can be nothing except being, for fate has bound it down to be whole and immobile Thus all (ideas) that men have set up, believing them to be true—birth and death, being and non-being, change of place, and alteration of bright hue—are mere words" (fragment 8, ed Diels), cf fragment 5, "thought (of being) and being are the same," fragment 6, "speech and thought must be real, for being exists and a naught does not exist," fragment 7, "non-being can never be proved to exist" Except in his view of Being as a sphere, Parmenides is in perfect accord with the Vedānta The similarity of Plato's doctrines is well known

§ 15 PHASES OF THE SELF—The highest existence is thus Thought without thinking, the state in which the soul has no consciousness of any external object, or indeed of any object at all, strictly speaking, for it is itself in conscious identity with the sum of all being or Universal Idea, "whilst he seeth not a thing, yet doth he see, though he see not the thing erstwhile to be seen He that hath sight loseth not his sight, for it is imperishable. But there is naught beside him, naught apart from him, that he may see" (B A iv iii 23)

The only analogy that experience furnishes for this supposed condition of soul is that of dreamless sleep, and it was inferred that in such sleep the soul is actually in this transcendent state

Besides this, the earlier Upanishads recognise two other states of the soul, waking and dreaming When awake the soul puts forth out of itself a world of sense and organs of sense and empirical thought, and renders itself the subject of the experiences conjured up by them In dreaming sleep the sense-organs swoon away and are absorbed into the *manas*, the organ forming the centre of empirical cognition and will (§ 18), which thus has now the vision of the world as it is reflected from the waking state, at the same time the "life-breaths," *prānas*, are active as in waking

The later Upanishads assume yet another phase, which they call the "Fourth" (*turīya*, *chaturtha*) In this the soul, transcending dreamless sleep, is absolutely wakeful in its union with the universal subject of thought, and exercises in perfect stillness an infinite real consciousness of all in the Self which is different in kind from the "unconscious consciousness" ascribed to dreamless sleep

The waking, dreaming, and dreamless phases are respectively termed *Vaiśvānara* ("common to all mankind"), *Taijasa* ("luminous," for in dreams the soul is its own light, B A iv iii 9), and *Prājna* ("intelligent," for in deep sleep the Self is one with the Universal Idea or "intelligent Self," *prājna ātmā*, B A iv iii 21), these terms do not occur until Mānd iii ff On *dreaming sleep* see also B A ii i 18 (soul wanders about within the body), iv iii 9–14 (two accounts, in one of which soul leaves the body, while in the other it remains in it), iii 20 f, Ch viii x 2, Pra iv 2 f *Dreamless sleep*, B A iv iii 19–33, Ch viii vi 3, x-xi *Fourth State*, Mānd vii, Maiti vi 19, vii 11, Māndūkya-kārikā i 12–16, iii 33 f See also Sankara on Brahma-sūtra i iii 19 f, 40 f, iii ii 1 f Sankara, following Ch iv iii 3, holds that in deep sleep, in which the soul is in temporary identity with Brahma, the functions of sense, together with the *manas*, in which they are absorbed, are merged in the "breaths" travelling through the pericardium and veins (cf § 18), while the soul becomes one with the Brahma residing under "determinations" in the heart (in B A ii i 19, it rests in the pericardium, in Ch viii vi 3 in the veins) The statement of Ch viii xii 3, that "the Calm (*samprasāda*), rising from this body, wins to the Supreme Light, and shows itself in its own form, this is the highest spirit (*purusha*)," is taken by Sankara (on Brahma-sūtra iv iv 1 f) as referring to the soul not in dreamless sleep, but in its final release from the body after enlightenment (see § 24), this "own form" is the existence of the soul in its absolute selfhood, where there is no longer a distinction between individual and universal soul For the theories of the Vedānta after Śankara see above, § 12

§ 16 MĀYĀ —The word *māyā*, magic illusion, is commonly used in the later Vedānta to denote the phantom character of the phenomenal world, and in this sense it does not appear in the Upanishads until the Śvetāśvatara (IV 10) It is not found in the Brahma-sūtra, and hence the question has often been raised whether the idea denoted by it was actually present in the minds of the authors of the older Upanishads

That phenomena, even to the first principles under which they are cognised (space, time, and causality), are unreal relatively to Absolute Being, is a cardinal doctrine not only of the Upanishads but of all metaphysics Even the Vedic poets assert a real being of primal unity concealed behind the manifold of experience, and on this is founded the Upanishadic principle that the universe exists only in and by virtue of a World-Idea essentially identical with the individual consciousness This, however, is still far from the *māyā*-theory of the later Vedānta The authors of the older Upanishads were still much influenced by the realism of the Vedas, and it is therefore doubtful whether they could have agreed with the Vedantists who treat the world of experience as *absolutely* unreal, a mere phantom conjured up by the Self for its own delusion As typical of the Upanishadic attitude we may regard the theory of the Five Ātmās (§ 12) and the long passage of the Brihad-āranyaka (III VII 3 f) where the Self is described in detail as the *antar-yāmī*, or "inward controller," functioning as soul within matter as its body Their view was in the main somewhat as follows Phenomena are evolved from the Self, and hold their existence as *intelligibilia* in fee from the Self, with the knowledge of the Self they become known as phases of it, hence they are, to this extent, and no further, really existent (*satya*, B A I VI 3), provisionally true, although it is only ignorance of the Self that regards them as really independent of the Self and manifold The Upanishads on the whole conceive the empiric soul's ignorance as a negative force, an absence of light, with Śankara and the later Vedānta it is positive, a false light, a constructive illusion Brahma as cause of phenomena is in the Upanishads a *real* material, in Śankara's school an *unreal* material

The difficulties besetting Śankara when he endeavours to bring logical order into the vague idealism of the Upanishads are very serious On the one hand he maintains that the whole phenomenal world is unreal (*avastu*) As a magician (*māyāvī*) causes a phantom or wraith to issue from his person which has no real existence and by which the magician himself is entirely unaffected, so Brahma creates from himself a universe which is an utter phantom and nowise modifies his absolute existence His creative "powers" (which are real only when regarded from the standpoint of his creation, the world of finite subjects and objects) constitute the demiurgic principle of an empiric universe, which is, from its own standpoint, coextensive with him, whereas absolutely speaking it does not exist at all (see commentary on Brahma-sūtra, II 1 6, 9, etc, and above, § 9) On the other hand, the universe, phantom as it is, nevertheless is a fact of consciousness Illusion though it be, the illusion *is* This predicate of existence is the bond uniting it with its source, the truly existent, Brahma (on II 1 6) Brahma is absolute thought, the world is false thought, but the subject in both cases is the same, the thinking Self Thus *Māyā* denotes the sum of phenomena—or, as more narrowly defined by some later Vedantists, the sum of matter—as illusively conceived by the Self, it is the Ignorance which creates the phantom of a universe and of an individual ego by imposing its figments upon pure Thought (§ 12)

§ 17 Relation of Universal to Individual Soul —It is a first principle of the Upanishads that the numberless individual souls are really one with the Universal Self But how is this relation conceivable? To this question no answer is vouchsafed The older texts instead give us cosmogonic myths, which realistically depict a Universal Spirit creating the phenomenal world and then animating it as world-soul, and the latter they simply identify with the self of the individual, sometimes more pantheistically (Ch VI III), sometimes more idealistically (B A II IV 5, III IV 1, V 1, etc) But why should there be this division between the one Absolute Soul and the innumerable individual souls condemned to suffer the intellectual darkness and physical sorrows of embodied life? The Upanishads find a solution in their theory of *karma*, the acts done in previous births requiring further embodiment to work away their influence upon the soul This implies a *regressus ad infinitum*, as every act is the resultant of a former act, and this conclusion is cheerfully drawn by the later Vedānta, which thus avoids the necessity of explaining the "origin of evil" The older Upanishads, whose cosmogonies contradict this theory, simply avoid the question

The theory which begins to appear in a somewhat late Upanishad (the Maitrāyanīya), that the Soul conceives division and plurality in consequence of the delusive attractions of physical Nature, and hence assumes embodied form and comes under the influence of "works," is partly connected with the dualism of the Sānkhya school, and partly with the theory of "illusion" developed in the later Vedānta (see § 16) Sankara generally regards the universe itself, i e the aggregate of subjects and objects of experience, as created in order to furnish finite souls with experiences in recompense of previous "works", but the reason moving the Supreme Brahma to render himself an efficient and material cause of a universe distinct from himself, says Śankara, can only be motiveless *sport* (see commentary on Brahma-sūtra, II 1 33)

§ 18 ORGANISM OF SOUL —I *Upanishads* — Every organic being is a soul, according to the Upanishads, and the degree of its organic development is directly proportioned to the merits of its former works The highest therefore are the souls of gods and men The soul in its human embodiment exercises three classes of functions (1) the sense-organs (*indriya*), which in slumber or swoon become paralysed and merge themselves into (2) the organ of thought (*manas*), which converts the data of the sense-organs into conscious modes of thought and volition, and (3) the "breaths" (*prāna*), a term originally denoting all the functions of physical life, then those higher functions upon which generally depends all life, whether conscious or unconscious, and into which during sleep or swoon are merged the *manas* and the sense-organs already absorbed in the latter

The name *indriya* for the sense-organs appears first in Kath and Kau Other texts usually call them *prāna* (a collective term, from the supremacy of the *prāṇa*, or breath), and comprise under the name ordinarily breath, speech, sight, hearing, and *manas* (e g B A I iv 7) The same ten *indriyas* as in the later system occur first in B A II iv 11, IV v 12, which adds *manas* and heart (cf Pra IV 2) On *manas* as central function of cognition and action see B A I v 3, IV i 6, Ch VII iii f, Kath VI 7 The sense-organs are compared to horses drawing the car of the body, *manas* to their bridle, Kath III 3, in Maitr II 6 the organs of action are the horses, the organs of intelligence (see below) the reins, *manas* the driver On the immersion of organs with *manas* in *prāna* see especially B A IV iii 12, Ch VI viii 2, Pra IV 2 f The "breaths" are usually given as five, viz (1) *prāna* in the strict sense, which in B A and Ch denotes exspiration, and later exspiration and inspiration together, (2) *apāna*, in B A and Ch the inspiration, later the wind causing digestion in the bowels or evacuation, (3) *vyāna*, respiratory action connecting *prāna* and *apāna*, variously conceived, (4) *samāna*, sometimes the wind digesting food, sometimes connection between exspiration and inspiration, (5) *udāna*, which carries food and drink up and down (Maitr II 6) and guides the soul to Brahma in death and sleep (Pra III 7, IV 4)

II *Later Vedānta*—In the system of Sankara the gross body, subtle body (§ 19), *karmāśraya* (§ 20), and *prānas* are classed together as the "determinations" or *upādhis* by which the Self conceives itself as an individual soul (above, § 12) Whereas the gross body is abandoned on death, the other organisms travel in a potential form with the soul throughout all its births By the term *prāna* Sankara, following the old Upanishadic usage, designates not only the unconscious "breaths," but also the conscious *indriyas* The *indriyas* (the functional forces whence arise the material sense-organs) according to him comprise the five functions of action (viz speech, grasp, locomotion, generation, and excretion) and the five of *buddhi* or intelligence (viz sight, hearing, taste, touch, and smell), with which is associated the *manas* as their centre The *prānas*, or "breaths" in the strict sense are the five known in the Upanishads Śankara explains *prāna* as exspiration, *apāna* as inspiration, *vyāna* as the force maintaining life when both exspiration and inspiration are checked, *samāna* as the digestive force, and *udāna* as the current leading the soul from the body on death (on II IV 8 f) When death takes place, the *indriyas* sink into *manas*, this into the *prānas*, these into the individual soul (lodged in the heart), this into the "subtle body" (§ 19), which then starts on its wanderings Thus Śankara (on IV II 1 f) explains the statement of Ch VI VIII 6 that on death Speech is merged in *manas*, this into *prāna*, this into Heat, this into the Higher Godhead These words, he holds, mean that the potential functions of conscious sensation are merged into those of unconscious vitality, the latter into the individual soul, this again into the "Heat," i e the "subtle body," which conveys the soul through its wanderings See also §§ 12, 15

The later Vedānta (e g the Vedānta-sāra and the Ātma-viveka and Vākya-sudhā ascribed to Śankara) schematises the functions of empiric thought by dividing the *antah-karana*, its collective organisation, into *chitta*, *manas* (often loosely called *antah-karana*), *buddhi*, and *aham-kāra* To *chitta* it ascribes the function of passing notice, to *manas* that of deliberation, and to *buddhi* that of determination Sometimes also it uses *buddhi* as a general term denoting both *aham-kāra*, the conception of egoity, which is the agent in empiric mental action, and *manas*, the instrument of egoity, in the false identification of these functions with the Self or Spirit lies the root of phenomenal illusion

§ 19 THE SUBTLE BODY —According to the later Vedānta, the Soul in its wanderings from birth to birth is accompanied by the sense-organs and "breaths" as sums of potential faculties, and has for its vehicle the "subtle body," *sūkshma-śarīra* The latter consists of portions of the five elements in their higher suprasensual form, and thus is as it were a seed which on occasion grows by the accession of gross matter into a physical body

There is no clear evidence for the existence of

this idea in the Upanishads until the mention of a *linga* (the term used in the Sānkhya school for "subtle body") in B A iv iv 6, cf Kath vi 8, Śvet vi 9, Maitr vi 10 For Śankara's view see especially on Brahma-sūtra, iii i 1 f, iv ii 6 f The "subtle body" adheres to the soul until it attains perfect enlightenment and release in Brahma, the souls which never reach this goal are always attended by it

§ 20 KARMA —The propelling force which conducts the Soul with its potential functions through endless incarnations as man, god, beast, or vegetable, is the *karmāśraya*, the substrate of its *karma* or works By "work" is understood not only every act of will, and of body in obedience to will, but also every act of ideation in which the subject of thought posits a non-self in opposition to itself, for in this false duality begins the Will, desire, attachment of the soul to its fetters of finitude, and therewith moral blindness Every such act transforms itself into a positive force acting upon the soul, and demanding a corresponding requital of good for good and evil for evil in future experiences, and the sum of these forces at the end of each life determines the form of birth in the next incarnation [1]

[1] See especially B A iii ii 13 (probably the earliest assertion of this theory as a solution of the problem of moral character), iv iv 2–6, Ch iii xiv 1, Śankara on Brahma-sūtra, iii iv 11, iv ii 6, and above, § 6, below, § 24

§ 21 Freedom of Will —It follows that in so far as man shares in the empiric world his whole moral and physical life is at every instant strictly predestined But at the same time his Self is implicitly free, inasmuch as in essence it is one with the Absolute Brahma, no matter how it be empirically sunk in the phenomenal world, and as soon as he attains the knowledge of this fundamental unity which is itself salvation, his freedom is complete, he is the One Absolute Brahma, and beside him there exists no empiric world [1]

§ 22 God —These two ideas, empiric servitude to Works and transcendental freedom, leave little room for a Supreme God or moral guide of the experiences of souls The older texts practically ignore such a power, their polytheistic myths are merely echoes from the Veda, allegorically turned, and when they refer to a supreme deity they mean the higher Self within man Later authors, however, began occasionally to set up in theistic fashion a distinction between the Self within and the Self without This finally led to the conception of the later Vedānta, in which the Supreme Self, styled "the Lord" (*Īśvara*), is given the function of directing as efficient cause the course of "works," so that each comes to its

[1] *Predestination* for empiric life, B A III VIII 9, IV IV 5, Ch III XIV 1, VIII I 5, *Unconscious freedom of transcendental Self*, Ch VIII III 2, *Absolute freedom in enlightenment*, Ch. VII, XXV 2, VII I 6, V, 4

requital in due season and form, while the direct responsibility for all man's experiences is thrown upon the inward Self In other circles the same theistic current led to the identification of this Ātmā-God with one of the great popular deities, usually Vishnu or Śiva, and thus arose the great theologies, of which the most significant is the Bhagavad-gītā, a compromise between Upanishadic idealism, Sānkhya physics, and practical faith The first definite theism is in Kath II 20 (?), 23, III I, V 13, Mund III II 3, Īśa 8, Śvet III 20, IV–VI, etc Worship of Brahma-Ātmā is however frequently mentioned in the Upanishads It is an adoration of the Self either in its unqualified absoluteness (cf Ch III XIV 1, "Brahma in sooth is this All, it hath therein its beginning, end, and breath, so one should worship it in stillness"), or as allegorically typified by some physical force (see § 5), or as represented by the sacred syllable *Om* or *Aum*, upon which see especially Mānd and Pra V, which sets forth the three degrees of reward for meditation upon one, two, or three elements of this word, cf Śankara on Brahma-sūtra, I III 13 See also §§ 8, 24

Śankara (on Brahma-sūtra, II III 29) claims that wherever the Vedas and Upanishads represent the absolute Brahma under the form of "determinations" (§ 12), this is for the purpose of worship of Brahma as qualified Supreme, *saguna*, e g in Ch. III. XIV. The conception of the soul's relation to God as that of a servant to his master is justified by him (on II iii 43 f), inasmuch as Brahma by his supreme "determinations" regulates the activity of the empiric soul in the exercise of its inferior "determinations" He permits the worship of this "qualified Brahma," i e the Absolute conceived under the forms of empiric thought, but regards it as inferior in saving power to the true knowledge (see §§ 24, 25) The works of religion—ritual and devotion—are of value only as aids to enlightenment , they are not necessary, and after enlightenment is gained they lose all significance (on III iv 25 f , IV i 1 f)

§ 23 BRAHMA THE DESTROYER —As we saw, the Upanishads are full of cosmogonies inherited from Vedic religion , but apparently they have not yet arrived at the belief in a periodical course of alternate creation, maintenance, and dissolution of worlds which later became general in India The earlier texts several times describe Brahma or some cognate power as consuming his creatures separately , but a collective destruction is nowhere mentioned in them [1]

In the later Vedānta the theory of periodical cataclysms is formally accepted Again and again the universe is created, and after a time dissolved again into indiscrete potentiality , this cycle of birth and death is without beginning and

[1] See especially B A I ii 1, Ch I ix 1, Taitt III 1, Kaṭh II 25 Universal dissolution appears first in Śvet III 2, IV 1

without end (§ 12) In the intervals between destruction and the following creation the eternal Veda, with its Brāhmanas and Upanishads, rests as a potential force in the thought of Brahma, and at the beginning of creation the ideas contained in it serve as archetypes for the formation of all phenomena in the now emerging universe, and are revealed to inspired sages, its *karma-kānda* or practical section (the four Vedas and the bulk of the Brāhmanas) to guide men to ritual and consequent worldly welfare, its *jnāna-kānda* or theoretical section (chiefly the Upanishads) to teach them the true knowledge of Brahma

§ 24 SALVATION —I *Upanishads* —Release of the soul (*mukti, moksha*), which falls to the lot of the elect few, consists in enlightenment, intuitive vision of the eternal unity of the thinker's Self with Brahma, to which he has hitherto been blind When once this saving knowledge has been gained, the enlightened man is no longer under the power of "works" He has everything in himself, for he is one with the All, together with the false idea of a self distinct from the universal Self the forces of former works have vanished away, thus he has no desire and no pain, and can have none And when his soul has cast off the body, it will be reborn nevermore, it is united for ever with the Absolute Brahma See especially the fine exposition in B A IV II-IV, also Ch. VII XXVI 2, Taitt II 9, Kena 11-12,

Mund II ii 8, III ii 9, and Sankara on Brahma-sūtra, I i 4, III iv 1 f, IV i 13 f

II *Later Vedānta*—Sankara points out that this saving intuition is unattainable by effort of will or thought, it arises from the power of the inner self, the metaphysical ego within us, which from a theistic and therefore empiric standpoint may be conceived as personal God, " the Lord," or " qualified Brahma " (§§ 12, 22) This knowledge annuls not only all sins, but likewise all works, no matter whether good or bad, which have not yet begun to bear fruit in present experience The works however which are the cause of the present series of experience must continue in operation even after the attainment of enlightenment, until their power is exhausted, whereupon the soul leaves the flesh for ever, as the potter's wheel continues to run round for a while after the potter's hand has been removed, but this subsequent bodily experience no longer has any influence upon the soul The B A IV iv 6 teaches that, whereas on death the souls of those who have only exoteric knowledge or no knowledge at all go forth to continue in empiric conditions, the Self of the enlightened man does not " go out " (*na utkrāmanti*), but enters into Brahma, with entire annihilation of spatial conditions, its *upādhis* or " determinations " wholly vanish, and it is absorbed in abstract entirety into the abstract Brahma (on Brahma-sūtra III iii 30, IV ii 12 f) See § 15.

There has been much speculation upon the divisions of *karma* A common classification is that which divides it into *sanchita*, *prārabdha*, and *kriyamāna* The *sanchita* or "accumulated" *karma* is that which was created in former births and has not yet begun to operate upon the soul *Prārabdha* or "commenced" *karma* is that which has already begun to affect the soul *Kriyamāna* is "being made," that is, it is the activity of the present which will influence the soul in future births The intellectual illumination of perfect "Brahma-knowledge" annuls both *sanchita* and *kriyamāna*, only the *prārabdha* remains, and this exhausts itself mechanically by prolonging the sage's physical life until all influence of *karma* is spent, and his body then dies

The later Vedānta designates by the term *jīvan-mukti* the condition of the enlightened sage previous to death, while his *prārabdha* karma is exhausting itself, his subsequent condition is called *videha-mukti*, "emancipation in freedom from the body"

§ 25 The After Life —I *Upanishads* —Good deeds are requited, according to the Veda, in another world, the heaven of the gods and the fathers The Brāhmanas regard the heaven of the gods as a place of recompense for the good, and the abode of the fathers as a hell in which men are reborn to lives of suffering proportioned to their sins in this world Finally we meet the doctrine of transmigration definitively set forth in the Upanishads, by which retribution is effected, in part at any rate, by rebirth in this world

The fullest eschatological scheme in the Upanishads is given in the parallel passages Ch v iii-x, B A vi ii The first half of these sections (Ch v iii-ix, B A vi ii 1-14) sets forth the theory that on death the soul goes to heaven in a sublimated form, here allegorically styled "waters" and "faith" (a conception in which are united the two ideas of "subtle body" and "works"), and from heaven returns at once to earthly birth, being sacrificed by the gods successively in the fires of heaven, the atmosphere, earth, man, and woman Here there is no idea of requital in any world but this The further paragraphs expound a more complicated theory of requital both in the other world and here The souls of the sages who "worship Faith as their mortification in the woods" (they who have the saving knowledge) ascend by a series of stages which lead to the sun, thence to the moon, thence to the lightning, and thence to Brahma, the "supreme light," from which they never return This is the "Way of the Gods," *deva-yāna* The souls of those who do pious works in the village (but have not won full enlightenment and withdrawn from the world) rise by the "Way of the Fathers," *pitri-yāna*, which leads finally to the moon, where in the company of the gods they enjoy the full recompense of their good deeds, after this they pass down to honourable rebirth on earth through successive stages (ether, wind, smoke, mist, cloud, rain, vegetation, food, and seed) The sinful, according to Ch v x 7, have also a proportionate share in the joys of the moon, and are afterwards reborn in the forms of base animals or equally degraded races of men, according to B A this rebirth is immediate On the other hand the famous passage B A iv iv 2-6 knows only of rebirth in recompense

II *Later Vedānta*—Śankara's system in the main follows these doctrines He holds that the truly enlightened become immediately one with Brahma (§ 24) But those souls which are bound in the empirical world must accordingly pass through empirical spheres of recompense They who have the lower or exoteric knowledge and worship the "qualified Brahma" (§ 12) pass through the "Way of the Gods" to the paradise called the "world of Brahma", here according to their merits they either gain by degrees the saving knowledge which transports them for ever to the Absolute Brahma (*krama-mukti*), or else they have due enjoyment of heavenly bliss until their "works" have shrunk to a residue (*anuśaya*), whereupon they descend to honourable earthly incarnations They who have done pious works travel by the "Way of the Fathers" to the moon, where they share the pleasures of paradise with the gods, and thence in due time return to earth Those who have neither knowledge nor good works pass to hell, there to expiate their sins in part before rebirth in lower forms , and besides hell Sankara, following the obscure words of the Ch , admits a " third place " of punishment, viz rebirth as the lowest and most ephemeral animals (on Brahma-sūtra, III I 8 f)

When men of inferior knowledge or good works die, their sense-functions are merged into the *manas*, *manas* into " breaths," " breaths " into the individual soul, which together with the " subtle body " passes into the heart, of which the peak is now lit up (B A IV IV 2) , thence the soul of the man of lower knowledge travels out by the *sushumnā* (an imaginary vein leading to the top of the head) by the road of the sun's rays (Ch VIII VI 5), to the " Way of the Gods," but that of the man of good works issues by way of the other 100 chief veins of the body into the " Way of the Fathers " (on Brahma-sūtra IV II 17 f) On IV III 1 f Sankara endeavours to reconcile the discrepant lists of the stations in the " Way of the Gods " given in Ch IV XV 5, V X 1, B A VI II 15, and Kau I III , and points out that by their names are to be understood their presiding deities As regards the road of return to rebirth, he follows Ch V X 5 f and B A VI II 16 (on III I. 22 f).

PART II

SOME TEXTS OF THE VEDĀNTA

I Creation[1]

1 In the beginning this universe was Self alone, there was naught else open-eyed He bethought Himself "Now I will create worlds!"

He created these worlds—the Ocean, the Light, the Dead, the Waters That is the Ocean which is beyond the heaven, the heaven is its foundation The Light is the sky The Dead is the Earth, the Waters are those beneath

He bethought Himself "There are the worlds, now I will create world-wardens!" He drew from the waters Man,[2] and made him solid He brooded over him When he had been brooded over, his mouth burst asunder like an egg, from his mouth arose Speech, from speech Fire His nostrils burst asunder, from his nostrils arose the incoming Breath, from the

[1] Aitareya Upanishad, 1

[2] *Purusha*, see above, §§ 4, 5, 7

Breath Wind His eyes burst asunder, from his eyes arose Sight, from Sight the Sun His ears burst asunder, from his ears arose Hearing, from Hearing Space His skin burst asunder, from his skin arose hair, from the hair plants and trees His heart burst asunder, from his heart arose Mind, from Mind the Moon His navel burst asunder from his navel arose the outgoing Breath, from the Breath Death His secret parts burst asunder, from his secret parts arose seed, from seed the Waters

2 These gods, having been created, fell into this great ocean, this He gave over to Hunger and Thirst [1] They said to Him "Find out for us a dwelling-place in which we may rest and eat food" He brought them a cow They said "This is not enough for us" He brought them a horse They said, "This is not enough for us" He brought them a man They said "Well done, forsooth!" For man is in sooth well done He said to them "Enter, each according to your dwelling-places" So Fire, becoming Speech, entered his mouth, Wind, becoming the incoming Breath, entered his

[1] The cosmic powers, Fire, Wind, Sun, Space, Vegetation, Moon, Death, and Water (each of which is created from a corresponding function of the ideal Man) are in themselves powerless They sink back into the primitive waters, and suffer hunger and thirst, they must have a home in the real Man in order to be satisfied and active The forces of Nature exist only through and in the human subject

nostrils, the Sun, becoming Sight, entered his eyes, Space, becoming Hearing, entered his ears, the Plants and Trees, becoming hair, entered his skin, the Moon, becoming Mind, entered his heart, Death, becoming the outgoing Breath, entered his navel, the Waters, becoming seed, entered his secret parts

Hunger and Thirst said to Him "Find out for us a dwelling-place" He said to them "I give you a share with these gods, I make you partners with them" Therefore it is that whosoever be the godhead for whom an offering is taken, Hunger and Thirst are partners therein

3 He bethought Himself "There are the worlds and the world-wardens, now I will create for them Food"

He brooded over the waters, when they had been brooded over, there arose from the waters a shape The shape that arose was Food

When this was created, it sought to escape Him He sought to seize it with Speech, but could not, if He had seized it with Speech, one might have been filled with food through speaking only He sought to seize it with the incoming Breath, but could not, if He had seized it with the Breath, one might have been filled with food through breathing only He sought to seize it with the Eye, but could not, if He had seized it with the Eye, one might have been filled with food through sight only He sought to seize it with the Ear, but could not , if He had seized it with the Ear, one might have been filled with food through hearing only He sought to seize it with the Skin, but could not , if He had seized it with the Skin, one might have been filled with food through touch only He sought to seize it with the Mind, but could not , if He had seized it with the Mind, one might have been filled with food through thinking only He sought to seize it with the secret parts, but could not , if He had seized it with the secret parts, one might have been filled with food through excretion only He sought to seize it with the outgoing Breath, and He swallowed it It is the Wind that grasps Food, the Wind that wins Food [1]

He bethought Himself "How can this be without me ?" He bethought Himself "By what way shall I come in ?" He bethought Himself "If speaking is by speech, in-breathing by the in-breath, sight by the eye, hearing by the ear, touch by the skin, thinking by the mind, out-breathing by the out-breath, excretion by the secret parts, then who am I ?" [2]

He cleft asunder the crown of the head, and by that door came in This door is called the "cleft" , it makes for bliss [3]

[1] The outgoing breath, *apāna* probably is here identified with the function of digestion (p 43) The rest of the sentence is based upon a word-play

[2] For the answer to this question, see the next extract,

[3] See above, § 9

Three dwellings has He, and three dream-states—this is His dwelling, this His dwelling, this His dwelling [1]

Having been born, He surveyed living things "What is here," said He, "that one would call other [than Me]?" He saw man to be most utterly Brahma, and He said, "*idam adarśam*" ("I have seen it") Therefore He has the name *Idan-dra* His name is indeed *Idan-dra*, but him who is *Idan-dra* men call *Indra*,[2] in a dark manner, for the gods love what is dark

II Who am I? [3]

The heart, the mind, consciousness, comprehension, understanding, intelligence, wisdom, insight, resolution, thought, prudence, eagerness, memory, conception, power, life, desire, will—all these are names of the Intelligence This is Brahma, this is Indra, this is Prajā-pati, this is all the gods, the five great elements Earth, Wind, Ether, Water, and Light, the tiny creatures and they that are midway, the seeds of either kind, the creatures born from eggs, membranes, sweat,

[1] See above, §§ 12, 15. Brahma dwells in the eye during the waking state, in the mind during dreams, and in the heart during dreamless sleep

[2] *Indra* is a Vedic god of the first rank, hence by a word-play our writer identifies him with Brahma

[3] Aitareya Upanishad, iii

and sprouts, the horses, oxen, men, elephants, whatsoever is breathing, walking or flying, and whatso is motionless, all this is guided by intelligence, founded on intelligence The universe is guided by intelligence, founded on intelligence Intelligence is Brahma

III The World Within[1]

"Now within this town of Brahma[2] is a dwelling, a little lotus-flower, within this is a little space, what is therewithin men should inquire after, yea, should seek to know"

If they should say to him "Within this town of Brahma is a dwelling, a little lotus-flower, within this is a little space, what is found therewithin which men should inquire after, yea, should seek to know?"—

he shall say "Verily that space within the heart is as great as this Space, therein are lodged both heaven and earth, both fire and wind, both sun and moon, lightning and stars, what one hath here and what he hath not, all this is lodged therein"

If they should say to him "If all this is lodged in this town of Brahma, and all beings and all

[1] Chhāndogya Upanishad, viii 1 f

[2] The body, whose organs of sense are compared to gates, the king within is the soul, or Self, the lotus the heart

desires—what remains thereof when old age comes upon it, or it dissolves?"—

he shall say "This grows not old with his aging, nor is it smitten by slaying of him This is the true town of Brahma In it are lodged the Desires[1] It is the Self, free from evil, ageless, deathless, sorrowless, hungerless, thirstless, real of desire, real of purpose So they who depart without finding here the Self and these real Desires, walk not as they list in any worlds, but they who depart after finding here the Self and these real Desires, walk as they list in all worlds

These real Desires are covered over by Untruth, real as they are, Untruth is their covering Man here can see no more any of his folk who depart hence But when he goes *there*[2] he finds all—those of his folk who are living, and those who have departed, and whatever else he wins not for seeking For there those real Desires are that were covered over by Untruth It is as with men who, knowing not the ground, should walk again and again over a hidden treasure and find it not, even so all creatures,

[1] Namely, the knowledge and will of the absolute subject of thought, or true Self As such, those Desires are essentially infinite, their limitation arises from an external "Untruth," the finite conditions of the world of physical experience, which the thinker is able to cast off

[2] Namely, into his own heart, into the full consciousness of his selfhood,

coming to it day by day, find not this Brahma-world, for they are cast back by Untruth [1]

Now that perfect Peace, rising up from this body, enters into the Supreme Light and issues forth in its own semblance This is the Self," said he, "this is the deathless, the fearless, this is Brahma

Now the Self is the dyke holding asunder the worlds that they fall not one into another Over this dyke pass not day and night, nor old age, nor death, nor sorrow, nor good deeds, nor bad deeds All ills turn away thence, for this Brahma-world is void of ill Therefore in sooth the blind, after passing over this dyke is no more blind, the wounded no more wounded, the sick no more sick Therefore in sooth even Night after passing over this dyke issues forth as Day, for in this Brahma-world is everlasting light"

IV THE INFINITE I [2]

"Verily this All is Brahma It has therein its birth, end, breath, as such one should worship it in stillness

Verily man is made of will As is man's will

[1] They pass every day into dreamless sleep, the perfect union with Brahma in the heart, but they are not conscious of this union, and the condition of their existence causes it to be only temporary See above, § 15

[2] Chhāndogya Upanishad, iii 14

in this world, such he becomes on going hence , so let him frame the will

Made of mind, bodied in breath, shaped in light, real of purpose, ethereal of soul, all-working, all-desiring, all-smelling, all-tasting, grasping this All, speaking naught, heeding naught—this is my Self within my heart, smaller than a rice-corn, or a barley-corn, or a mustard-seed, or a canary-seed, or the pulp of a canary-seed—this is my Self within my heart, greater than earth, greater than sky, greater than heaven, greater than these worlds All-working, all-desiring, all-smelling, all-tasting, grasping this All, speaking naught, heeding naught—this is my Self within my heart, this is Brahma , to Him shall I win when I go hence He with whom it is thus has indeed no doubt" Thus spake Sāndilya

V Know Thy Self [1]

The world then was not yet unfolded It became unfolded in Name and Shape, so that one might say, "He of this or that name is of this or that shape" So even now it becomes unfolded in Name and Shape, so that one may say, "He of this or that name is of this or that shape" He[2] passed into it up to the nail-tips, as a razor might

[1] Bṛihad-āraṇyaka Upanishad, I iv 7–10
[2] Namely, the Self, or Brahma.

be laid in a razor-case or the All-Supporter[1] in the All-Supporter's nest They see Him not, for He is divided As breathing, He is called Breath, as speaking, Speech, as seeing, Sight, as hearing, Hearing, as thinking, Mind, these are the names for his workings A man who worships one or another thereof understands not, for He is but in division as one or another thereof So He should be worshipped as the Self, for therein do all these become one

This Self is the track of the universe, for by it is the universe known, yea, as a thing may be followed up by its track Fame and praise a man finds who has such knowledge

This Self is dearer than a son, dearer than substance, dearer than all beside, more inward If of a man who calls another than the Self dear it should be said that he will lose his darling, it may well come to pass He should worship the Self only as darling, for him who worships the Self as darling his darling perishes not

They say "Seeing that men deem that by knowledge of Brahma they shall become the universe, what did Brahma know that He became the universe?"

The world forsooth was in the beginning Brahma It knew *itself*, "I am Brahma", therefore it became the universe And whosoever of the gods understood this also became the same,

[1] The Fire-God

likewise of sages and of men Seeing this, the sage Vāmadeva set it forth, saying "I have become Manu and the Sun"[1] So now likewise he who knows "I am Brahma" becomes the universe The very gods have no power that he should not be so, for he becomes the Self of them

Now he who worships another godhead, saying "This is not the same as I," understands not, he is as it were a beast belonging to the gods Even as many beasts profit a man, so each man profits the gods It is unpleasing when one beast is taken away, how much more when many are taken! Therefore it is not pleasing to them[2] that men should know this

VI PARABLES[3]

"If one should smite upon the root of this great tree, beloved, it would sweat sap, and live If one should smite upon its midst, it would sweat sap, and live If one should smite upon its top, it would sweat sap, and live Instinct with the Live Self, it stands full lush and glad

But if the Live One leave one bough, it withers If it leave another bough, it withers If it leave a third bough, it withers If it leave the whole, the whole withers So know, beloved," said he,

[1] Rig-veda, IV XXVI 1 [2] Namely to the gods
[3] Chhāndogya Upanishad, VI XI-XIII

"the thing whence the Live One has departed does indeed die, but the Live One dies not In this subtleness has this All its essence, it is the True, it is the Self, thou art it, Śvetaketu"

"Let my lord teach me further"

"Be it so, beloved," said he

"Bring from yonder a fig"

"Here it is, my lord"

"Break it"

"It is broken, my lord"

"What seest thou in it?"

"Here are but little seeds, my lord"

"Now break one of them"

"It is broken, my lord"

"What seest thou in it?"

"Naught whatsoever, my lord"

And he said to him: "Of that subtleness which thou canst not behold, beloved, is this great fig-tree made Have faith, beloved In this subtleness has this All its essence, it is the True, it is the Self, thou art it, Śvetaketu"

"Let my lord teach me further"

"Be it so, beloved," said he

"Lay this salt in water, and on the morrow draw nigh to me" And he did so Then he said to him "Bring me the salt which thou laidst in the water yester eve"

He felt, but found it not, it was as melted away

"Drink from this end thereof How is it?"

"It is salty"

"Drink from the midst How is it?"

"It is salty"

"Drink from yonder end How is it?"

"It is salty"

"Lay it aside, and draw nigh to me" And he did so

"It is still present," said he to him, "herein forsooth thou canst not behold Being, beloved, but herein soothly it is In this subtleness has this All its essence, it is the True, it is the Self, thou art it, Śvetaketu"

VII The Soul in Sleep[1]

"What is the Self?"

"It is the Spirit[2] made of understanding among the Breaths, the inward light within the heart, that walks abroad, abiding the same, through both worlds[3] He meditates, as it were, He hovers about, as it were Turned to sleep, He passes beyond this world, the shapes of death

This Spirit at birth enters into the body, and is

[1] Bṛihad-āraṇyaka Upanishad, iv iii 7–33

[2] *Purusha*, see above p 56

[3] Namely, this world in waking and dreaming, and the world of Brahma in deep sleep or death.

blent with evils, at death He passes out, and leaves evils

Two seats has this Spirit, this and the seat in the world beyond[1], and midway is a third, the seat of dreams Standing in this midway seat, He looks upon these two seats, this and the seat in the world beyond Now as this is a step toward the seat in the world beyond, He makes this step and beholds both evils and delights

When He sleeps, He takes matter from this all-containing world, Himself hews it down, Himself builds it up, and sleeps in His own brightness, His own light Here the Spirit has Self for light

Therein are no cars, no car-teams, no roads, but He creates cars, car-teams, roads Therein are no joys, mirths, merriments, but He creates joys, mirths, merriments Therein are no pools, lakes, streams, but He creates pools, lakes, streams For He is the maker

When in this dreaming He has wantoned and wandered, and seen good and evil, He hastens back according to His entrance and His place to the bound of waking He is followed by naught of all that He has seen there, for to this Spirit nothing clings

[1] The soul's seats are (1) that in this world, and (2) that in the transcendental "Brahma-world," which it visits on death The former is the site of sorrows, the latter of pure joy Between these is the condition of sleep, for dreaming sleep is still in touch with waking experience, and dreamless sleep is a temporary approach towards the "Brahma-world"

When in this waking He has wantoned and wandered, and seen good and evil, He hastens back according to His entrance and His place to the bound of dreams   Even as a great fish passes along both banks, on this side and on yonder side, so this Spirit passes along both bounds, the bound of dreaming and the bound of waking

But as a falcon or an eagle, when it is wearied with flying about in yonder sky, folds its wings and sets itself to couch down, so this Spirit hastens toward that bound wherein He sleeps desiring no desire, beholding no dream   Whatever waking terror He sees [in dreams], when men seem to smite Him or to oppress Him, when an elephant seems to crush Him, or He seems to fall into a ditch, this in His ignorance He deems true   But when like a god, like a king, He thinks "I am this All, universal," this is the highest world for Him

This is His shape wherein He is beyond desire, free from ill, fearless   As when a man embraced by his beloved knows naught of whatsoever is without or within, so this Spirit embraced by the Self of Intelligence knows naught of what is without or within [1]   This is His shape wherein desire is won, desire is of Self, desire is not, grief is gone   Herein the father is no father, the mother no mother, the worlds no worlds, the Gods no

[1] In dreamless sleep the individual consciousness is merged into universal consciousness, *prājna ātmā* or "Self of Intelligence," and thus arises absolute unconsciousness

Gods, the Vedas no Vedas, herein the thief is no thief, the murderer no murderer, the Chāndāla no Chāndāla, the Paulkasa no Paulkasa,[1] the beggar-monk no beggar-monk, the ascetic no ascetic Good attaches not, evil attaches not, for then has He overpast all griefs of the heart

While He sees not, yet without seeing He sees, the sight of the seer is not to be broken, for it is imperishable But there is naught beside Him, naught apart from Him, that He should see When He understands not, yet without understanding He understands, the understanding of the understander is not to be broken, for it is imperishable But there is naught beside Him, naught apart from Him, that He should understand

If there should be as it were another, one would see another, smell another, taste another, speak to another, hear another, think of another, feel another, understand another

The Seer is the Waters,[2] one with naught beside He is the Brahma-world, O king" Thus did Yājnavalkya teach him "This is the highest way for Him, this the highest fortune for Him,

[1] Two of the basest castes

[2] This may refer to an Indian theory according to which water is essentially tasteless, but derives its special flavour from its surroundings, as in a cocoanut or a lemon (see Sānkhya-kārikā, xvi), or perhaps it is based upon the Vedic theory that made water the first principle of cosmic being, as in the doctrine of Thales of Miletus

this the highest world for Him, this the highest bliss for Him, of this bliss other creatures live on but a morsel"

VIII GĀRGĪ AND YĀJNAVALKYA[1]

"Yājnavalkya," said she, "as a warrior from the land of Kāśi or Videha might string his unstrung bow and come forward holding in his hand two arrows to pierce through his foe, even so I have come forward against thee with two questions, answer me them"

"Ask, Gārgī"

"Yājnavalkya," said she, "that which is above the heavens, which is beneath the earth, which is midway between the heavens and the earth, which they call *What hath been, What is,* and *What shall be*—in what is it woven and woofed?"

"Gārgī," said he, "that which is above the heavens, which is below the earth, which is midway between the heavens and the earth, which they call *What hath been, What is,* and *What shall be,* is woven and woofed in the ether"

"Homage to thee, Yājnavalkya," said she "for thou hast answered me this, make ready for the other"

"Ask, Gārgī"

[1] Bṛihad-āraṇyaka Upanishad, III viii 2–11.

"Yājnavalkya," said she, "that which is above the heavens, which is below the earth, which is midway between the heavens and the earth, which they call *What hath been*, *What is*, and *What shall be*—in what is it woven and woofed?"

"Gārgī," said he, "that which is above the heavens, which is below the earth, which is midway between the heavens and the earth, which they call *What hath been*, *What is*, and *What shall be*, is woven and woofed in the ether"

"And in what is the ether woven and woofed?"

"Gārgī," said he, "that is what Brahmans call the Unfading, it is not gross, not fine, not short, not long, not red, not fluid, not shadow, not darkness, not wind, not ether, not clinging, without taste, without smell, without eye, without ear, without speech, without mind, without vital force, without breath, without mouth, without measure, without aught inward, without aught outward, it consumes nothing, none consumes it At the behest of the Unfading, Gārgī, sun and moon are held asunder, at the behest of the Unfading, Gārgī, heaven and earth are held asunder, at the behest of the Unfading, Gārgī, minutes, hours, days and nights, fortnights, months, seasons, and years are held asunder, at the behest of the Unfading, Gārgī, flow the rivers, some eastward from the white mountains, some westward, each in its own way At the behest of the Unfading, Gārgī, men praise givers, the Gods hang upon the sacrifice-giver, the Fathers upon the ladle Indeed, Gārgī, to him who makes oblation and sacrifice, and mortifies himself in this world for many thousands of years without knowing the Unfading, it comes to an end Indeed, Gārgī, he who departs from this world without knowing the Unfading is wretched But he who departs from this world knowing the Unfading, Gārgī, is the Brahman Indeed, Gārgī, the Unfading unseen sees, unheard hears, unthought thinks, uncomprehended comprehends There is naught else than this which sees, naught else that hears, naught else that thinks, naught else that comprehends In the Unfading, forsooth, Gārgī, is the ether woven and woofed "

IX THE EVERLASTING NAY [1]

Verily this great unborn Self it is that is compact of understanding amid the life-breaths, that lies in the ether within the heart, master of all, lord of all, ruler of all , He becomes not greater by a good deed nor less by an ill deed , He is king of all, ruler of born beings, guardian of born beings, the dyke holding asunder these worlds that they fall not one into another Brahmans seek to know Him by reading the Veda, by sacrifice, by charity, by mortification Knowing

[1] Bṛihad-āraṇyaka Upanishad, IV IV 22–23

Him, a man becomes a saint, wandering friars wander forth seeking Him for their world Understanding this, the ancients desired not offspring "What is offspring to us who have this Self for this world?" So having departed from desire of sons, from desire of substance, and desire of the world, they went about begging For desire of sons is desire of substance, desire of substance is desire of the world, these are both desires

This Self is *Nay*, *Nay* not to be grasped, for He is not grasped, not to be broken, for He is not broken, unclinging, for He clings not, He is not bound, He trembles not, He takes no hurt One [who knows this] is overcome neither by having done evil for His sake nor by having done good for His sake, he overcomes both, work done and work not done grieve him not

This is said by a verse

The Brahman's constant majesty by works
Nor waxes more, nor wanes This shall he
  trace,
This known, ill deeds defile him nevermore

X The Spirit Within[1]

Then Uddālaka Āruṇi[2] questioned him "Yājnavalkya," said he, "we dwelt among

[1] Bṛihad-āraṇyaka Upanishad, III vii

[2] A patronymic, meaning "son of Aruṇa"

the Madras, in the house of Patanchala Kāpya,[1] studying sacrifice He had a wife who was possessed by a spirit[2], we asked him who he was, and he answered that he was Kabandha Ātharvana, and said to Patanchala Kāpya and to the students of sacrifice, "Knowest thou, Kāpya, that Thread whereby this world and the world beyond and all creatures are bound together?" "Nay, my lord," said Patanchala Kāpya, "I know it not" Then he said to Patanchala Kāpya and the students of sacrifice, "Knowest thou, Kāpya, that Inward Ruler who rules inwardly this world and the world beyond and all creatures?" "Nay, my lord," said Patanchala Kāpya, "I know him not" Then he said to Patanchala Kāpya and the students of sacrifice, "Verily, Kāpya, he who should know that Thread and that Inward Ruler knows Brahma, knows the worlds, knows the Vedas, knows the creatures, knows the Self, knows the All" This he said to them this I know If thou, Yājnavalkya, shalt drive home the Brahman's cows without knowing that Thread and that Inward Ruler, thy head shall split"[3]

[1] A patronymic signifying a descendant of Kapi Similarly *Ātharvana*, below, means a descendant of the mythical sage Atharvan

[2] In Sanskrit *Gandharva*, originally, perhaps, the Gandharvas were spirits of fertility, but in classical literature they are a kind of fairies, with musical proclivities See especially Pischel and Geldner, *Vedische Studien*, vol i, p 183 foll

[3] This dialogue between Uddālaka and Yājnavalkya forms

"Verily, Gautama, I know that Thread and that Inward Ruler"

"Any man may say, 'I know, I know', but do thou say how thou knowest"

"Truly, Gautama," said he, "the wind is that Thread, for by the wind as thread, Gautama, this world and the world beyond and all creatures are bound together Therefore, Gautama, they say of a man who has died that his limbs are relaxed, for by the wind as thread, Gautama, were they bound together"

"It is so, Yājnavalkya Tell of the Inward Ruler"

"He who, dwelling in the earth, is other than the earth, whom the earth knows not, whose body the earth is, who inwardly rules the earth, is thy Self, the Inward Ruler, the deathless He who, dwelling in the waters, is other than the waters, whom the waters know not, whose body the waters are, who inwardly rules the waters, is thy Self, the Inward Ruler, the deathless He who, dwelling in the fire, is other than the fire, whom the fire knows not whose body the fire is, who inwardly rules the fire, is thy Self, the

part of a disputation between Brahman theologians, as the prize of which a thousand cows were offered by King Janaka of Videha (Bṛihad-ār Up iii i 1) The mention of a splitting head occurs several times in a similar connection in the Upanishads, practically it means that he who accepts the challenge and fails in these tourneys of wit is doomed to death by "visitation of God"

Inward Ruler, the deathless He who, dwelling in the sky, is other than the sky, whom the sky knows not, whose body the sky is, who inwardly rules the sky, is thy Self, the Inward Ruler, the deathless He who, dwelling in the wind, is other than the wind, whom the wind knows not, whose body the wind is, who inwardly rules the wind, is thy Self, the Inward Ruler, the deathless He who, dwelling in the heavens, is other than the heavens, whom the heavens know not, whose body the heavens are, who inwardly rules the heavens, is thy Self, the Inward Ruler, the deathless He who, dwelling in the sun, is other than the sun, whom the sun knows not, whose body the sun is, who inwardly rules the sun, is thy Self, the Inward Ruler, the deathless He who, dwelling in space, is other than space, whom space knows not, whose body space is, who inwardly rules space, is thy Self, the Inward Ruler, the deathless He who, dwelling in moon and stars, is other than moon and stars, whom moon and stars know not, whose body moon and stars are, who inwardly rules moon and stars, is thy Self, the Inward Ruler, the deathless He who, dwelling in the ether, is other than the ether, whom the ether knows not, whose body the ether is, who inwardly rules the ether, is thy Self, the Inward Ruler, the deathless He who, dwelling in the dark, is other than the dark, whom the dark knows not, whose body the dark is, who inwardly rules the dark, is thy Self, the Inward Ruler, the deathless He who, dwelling in the light, is other than the light, whom the light knows not, whose body the light is, who inwardly rules the light, is thy Self, the Inward Ruler, the deathless Thus as to godhead, now as to nature He who, dwelling in all beings, is other than all beings, whom all beings know not, whose body all beings are, who inwardly rules all beings, is thy Self, the Inward Ruler, the deathless Thus as to nature, now as to personality He who, dwelling in the breath, is other than the breath, whom the breath knows not, whose body the breath is, who inwardly rules the breath, is thy Self, the Inward Ruler, the deathless He who, dwelling in speech, is other than speech, whom speech knows not, whose body speech is, who inwardly rules speech, is thy Self, the Inward Ruler, the deathless He who, dwelling in the eye, is other than the eye, whom the eye knows not, whose body the eye is, who inwardly rules the eye, is thy Self, the Inward Ruler, the deathless. He who, dwelling in the ear, is other than the ear, whom the ear knows not, whose body the ear is, who inwardly rules the ear, is thy Self, the Inward Ruler, the deathless He who, dwelling in the mind, is other than the mind, whom the mind knows not, whose body the mind is, who inwardly rules the mind, is thy Self, the Inward Ruler, the deathless He who, dwelling in the skin, is other than the skin, whom the skin knows not, whose body the skin is, who inwardly rules the skin, is thy Self, the Inward Ruler, the deathless He who, dwelling in the understanding, is other than the understanding, whom the understanding knows not, whose body the understanding is, who inwardly rules the understanding, is thy Self, the Inward Ruler, the deathless He who, dwelling in the seed, is other than the seed, whom the seed knows not, whose body the seed is, who inwardly rules the seed, is thy Self, the Inward Ruler, the deathless He unseen sees, unheard hears, unthought thinks, uncomprehended comprehends There is no other than he who sees, no other who hears, no other who thinks, no other who comprehends He is thy Self, the Inward Ruler, the deathless All else is fraught with sorrow"

Then Uddālaka Āruṇi held his peace

XI THE WISDOM OF RAIKVA[1]

Jānaśruti Pautrāyana was a devout giver, bestowing much largesse, preparing much food He caused lodgings to be built everywhere, that he might have men everywhere fed Now in the night there flew swans by One swan said to another, "Ho, ho, Dim-eye, Dim-eye! Jāna-

[1] Chhāndogya Upanishad, IV 1–3

śruti Pautrāyana's splendour is outspread like that of the heavens, so touch it not, lest thou burn thyself"

The other answered him, "Who forsooth is he of whom thou speakest as though he were Raikva of the Cart?"

"What meanest thou by Raikva of the Cart?"

"As the lower dice-throws fall under the winning four-throw, so whatsoever good deed the people do falls to him, of him who knows this and of that which he knows do I speak"[1]

Jānaśruti Pautrāyana overheard this When he rose up, he said to his chamberlain, "Ho, thou speakest as of Raikva of the Cart[2], what meanest thou by Raikva of the Cart?"

"As the lower dice-throws fall under the winning four-throw, so whatsoever good deed the people do falls to him, of him who knows this and of that which he knows do I speak"

The chamberlain sought [Raikva], and came back, saying "I have found him not" [Jānaśruti] said to him, "Ho, go for him in the place where a Brahman is to be sought"

[1] The Hindus know of four casts of the dice—the *kṛita*, counting as four, the *tretā*, counting as three, the *dvapara*, counting as two, and the *kali*, reckoned as one, the *krita* outweighs all the other throws, and hence has the value of 10 Raikva has universal wisdom, hence the virtues of all other men are merely parts of his excellence, which includes them all

[2] The chamberlain, after Hindu custom, had addressed him in strains of panegyric on his rising from bed

[Raikva] was under a waggon, scratching his scabs, and he[1] sat down before him, and said to him, "Art thou Raikva of the Cart, my lord?"

"Yea, I am," he answered

The chamberlain came back, saying, "I have found him"

Then Jānaśruti Pautrāyana took six hundred kine, a golden chain, and a mule-car, and drew near to him, and said, "Raikva, here are six hundred kine, a golden chain, and a mule-car, my lord, teach me the deity that thou worshippest"

But the other answered, "Fie on thee, base fellow, keep them for thyself, with thy kine!"

Then Jānaśruti Pautrāyana took a thousand kine, a golden chain, a mule-car, and his daughter, and drew near to him, and said, "Raikva, here are a thousand kine, a golden chain, a mule-car, a wife, and the village in which thou art sitting, my lord, teach me!"

He lifted up her face, and said, "He has brought these! Base fellow, with this face alone thou mightest have made me speak"

That is the place called Raikva-parna in the land of the Mahāvrishas where he dwelt at his bidding

Thus he said to him

"The Wind in sooth is an ingatherer When fire goes out, it sinks into the Wind When the sun goes down, it sinks into the Wind When

[1] The chamberlain of Jānaśruti

the moon goes down, it sinks into the Wind When waters dry up, they sink into the Wind For the Wind gathers in all these Thus as to godhead

Now as to personality The Breath is an ingatherer[1] When one sleeps, the speech sinks into the Breath, the eye into the Breath, the ear into the Breath, the mind into the Breath For the Breath gathers in all these These are the two ingatherers, the Wind among the gods and the Breath among the breaths

A Brahman-student begged alms of Śaunaka Kāpeya and Abhipratāri Kākshaseni when their meal was set before them They gave him nothing He said

"Who is the one God, guardian of the world,
Who swallowed up the other mighty four?
On him, Kāpeya, mortals may not look,
Abhipratāri, many are his homes
To him forsooth who has this food it is not given"

Then Śaunaka Kāpeya, having pondered, answered him thus

"The spirit of the Gods, the creatures' sire,
Golden of tooth and greedy he, nor witless
Exceeding is his majesty, they say,
For he uneaten eats what none may eat

"So this is what we worship, O Brahman-

[1] See § 18.

student Give him alms!" And they gave to him

These in sooth are the ten, five and five[1], this is the four-throw Therefore the ten, the four-throw, are in all parts of the world as food This is Virāt, eater of food, thereby all the world is seen All the world is seen by him, he becomes an eater of food, who has this knowledge"

XII SATYAKĀMA[2]

Satyakāma Jābāla thus addressed his mother Jabālā "I would keep the term of Brahman-studentship, madame, of what family am I?"

She said to him "I know not, child, of what family thou art I got thee in my youth, when I was much busied in doing service I myself know not of what family thou art But I am named Jabālā, thou art named Satyakāma, call thyself then Satyakāma Jābāla"[3]

[1] The first five are wind, fire, sun, moon, and water, in the cosmos, the second five are breath, speech, eye, ear, and mind, in the microcosm Wind and Breath are the final principles of being He who knows himself to be identical with Wind and Breath, and thus becomes himself the highest principle, gathers to himself all the nourishing powers of nature These ten natural forces are typified by the four-throw in dice, which counts as ten, and by Virāṭ, which is both the name of a metre of ten syllables and a mythological figure symbolic of primitive matter

[2] Chhāndogya Upanishad, iv 4-9

[3] In default of a father's name, that of his mother is to serve our hero to form his patronymic

He went to Hāridrumata Gautama and said "I would keep the term of Brahman-studentship with thee, sir, let me come to thee, sir"

He said to him "Of what family art thou, beloved?"

"I know not, sir," said he, "of what family I am I asked my mother, and she answered me saying, 'I got thee in my youth, when I was much busied in doing service, I myself know not of what family thou art, but I am named Jabālā, thou art named Satyakāma' So I am myself Satyakāma Jābāla, sir"

He said to him "None but a Brahman can speak out thus Bring the faggots,[1] beloved I will receive thee, thou hast not departed from truth"

When he had received him, he set aside four hundred lean and feeble cows, and said "Herd thou these, beloved"* As he drove them forth, [Satyakāma] said "I will not return but with a thousand" He stayed away some years, then when they had grown to a thousand, a bull said to him, "Satyakāma!" "Sir!" he answered

"We have come to a thousand, beloved, take us to the master's homestead I will tell thee a quarter of Brahma"

[1] Used in the ceremony of the reception (*upanayana*) of the Brahman-student (*brahma-chāri*) by the teacher in whose house he was henceforth to lodge

"Tell me, sir"

And he said to him "The eastern region is a sixteenth, the western region a sixteenth, the southern region a sixteenth, the northern region a sixteenth This, beloved, is a quarter of Brahma, in four sixteenths, and called The Brilliant He who with such knowledge worships this quarter of Brahma in four sixteenths as The Brilliant, becomes brilliant in this world, brilliant worlds he wins who with such knowledge worships this quarter of Brahma in four sixteenths as The Brilliant The Fire will tell thee a quarter"

In the morning he drove out the cows When they came home at evening, he laid a fire, closed in the cows, laid on fuel, and sat down facing the east westward of the fire

The Fire said to him, "Satyakāma!"

"Sir!" he answered

"I will tell thee a quarter of Brahma, beloved"

"Tell me, sir"

And he said to him "The earth is a sixteenth, the sky a sixteenth, the heaven a sixteenth, the ocean a sixteenth This, beloved, is a quarter of Brahma, in four sixteenths, and called The Boundless He who with such knowledge worships this quarter of Brahma in four sixteenths as The Boundless, becomes boundless in this world, boundless worlds he wins who with such knowledge worships this quarter of Brahma in four sixteenths as The Boundless The Swan will tell thee a quarter"

In the morning he drove out the cows When they came home at evening, he laid a fire, closed in the cows, laid on fuel, and sat down facing the east westward of the fire A swan flew towards him and said, "Satyakāma!" "Sir!" he answered

"I will tell thee a quarter of Brahma, beloved"

"Tell me, sir"

And he said to him "Fire is a sixteenth, the sun a sixteenth, the moon a sixteenth, the lightning a sixteenth This, beloved, is a quarter of Brahma, in four sixteenths, and called The Lustrous He who with such knowledge worships this quarter of Brahma in four sixteenths as The Lustrous, becomes lustrous in this world, lustrous worlds he wins who with such knowledge worships this quarter of Brahma in four sixteenths as The Lustrous The madgu-bird will tell thee a quarter"

In the morning he drove out the cows When they came home at evening, he laid a fire, closed in the cows, laid on fuel, and sat down facing the east westward of the fire A madgu-bird flew towards him and said, "Satyakāma!" "Sir!" he answered

"I will tell thee a quarter of Brahma, beloved"

"Tell me, sir"

And he said to him "The breath is a sixteenth, the eye a sixteenth, the ear a sixteenth, the mind a sixteenth This, beloved, is a quarter of Brahma, in four sixteenths, and called The Spacious He who with such knowledge worships this quarter of Brahma in four sixteenths as The Spacious, becomes spacious in this world, spacious worlds he wins who with such knowledge worships this quarter of Brahma in four sixteenths as The Spacious"

He came to the master's homestead The master said to him, "Satyakāma!" "Sir!" he answered

"Thou art bright, beloved, as one who knows Brahma Who has taught thee?"

"Other than men," he answered, "but prithee do thou tell it to me, sir For I have heard from men like thee, sir, that knowledge learned from a master is the best guide"

He told him thereof, and naught of it was lost

XIII Light and Darkness[1]

In the Lord is to be veiled this universe, whatsoever stirs in the world With renunciation thereof[2] thou mayst enjoy, lust thou after the wealth of none

[1] The Iśāvāsya or Vājasaneyi-samhitā Upanishad
[2] Viz of the phenomenal world of sense-perception

One may seek to live a hundred years doing works here So it is with thee, not otherwise , his work defiles not man [1]

Dæmonic are in sooth these worlds, veiled in blind darkness , into them pass after death whatsoever folk slay their own souls

The One, unstirring, is yet swifter than the mind , the gods cannot reach it as it travels before Standing it outspeeds others that run , in it the Wind-spirit lays the waters

It stirs, and stirs not , it is far, and near It is within all, and outside all that is

But he who discerns all creatures in his Self, and his Self in all creatures, has no disquiet thence

What delusion, what grief can be with him in whom all creatures have become the very self of the thinker discerning their oneness ?

He has spread around, a thing bright, bodiless, taking no hurt, sinewless, pure, unsmitten by evil , a sage, wise, encompassing, self-existent, he has duly assigned purposes for all time

Into blind darkness pass they who worship Ignorance , into still greater dark they who are content with Knowledge [2]

It is neither what comes by Knowledge, they

[1] Provided he has knowledge of Brahma

[2] "Ignorance" probably means the conception of the phenomenal world as really existent in itself , "Knowledge," the attempt to trace the universe back to a first principle different from the Self

say, nor what comes by Ignorance, thus have we heard from the sages who taught us this lore

He who understands both Knowledge and Ignorance[1] passes by Ignorance over death and by Knowledge enjoys deathlessness

Into blind darkness pass they who worship Change-into-naught, into still greater dark they who worship Change-into-aught[2]

It is neither what comes by Change-into-aught, they say, nor what comes by Change-into-naught, thus have we heard from the sages who taught us this lore

He who understands[3] both Change-into-aught and Destruction passes by Destruction over death and by Change-into-aught enjoys deathlessness

The face of truth is covered with a golden bowl O Pūshan, remove it, that the keeper of truths may see[4]

O Pūshan, sole seer, O Yama, Sun, child of

[1] Viz he who knows both these forms of knowledge to be delusive

[2] The author here attacks those who believe that Being undergoes change either into non-being or into a different phase of being His cardinal principle is that Being is one and changeless

[3] I e, he who knows both ideas to be false

[4] This and the following verses (a death-bed prayer, according to tradition) are a prayer to the Sun-god to reveal the figure of the *Purusha* in the sun (corresponding to the figure in the human eye, and symbolic of Brahma, see p 16) The Sun-god is here identified with Yama, the ruler of the dead On Prajā-pati, see p 14, in the next extract he is mythically represented as a teacher of philosophic lore

Prajā-pati, part asunder thy rays, mass together thy radiance I see that fairest shape of thee Yonder, yonder spirit am I

The breath to the everlasting wind, and be this body ended in ashes

Om! remember, O my spirit, remember the work! remember, O my spirit, remember the work! O Fire, lead us by good ways to riches, thou god who knowest all courses, keep far from us crooked sin, and we will offer to thee exceeding homage and praise[1]

XIV THE FALSE AND THE TRUE[2]

"The Self, free from evil, ageless, deathless, sorrowless, hungerless, thirstless, real of desire, real of purpose, this should men inquire after, yea, should seek to know All worlds he wins and all desires who traces out and understands the Self," said Prajā-pati

Both the gods and the demons marked this "Come," said they, "let us seek out this Self by seeking out which one wins all worlds and all desires" So Indra of the gods and Virochana of the demons set out on a travel, and without being in compact they both came with faggots

[1] This verse is Rig-veda, i 189, i

[2] Chhāndogya Upanishad, VIII vii-xii

in their hands[1] to Prajā-pati, and stayed as Brahmaṇ-students for two-and-thirty years

Then said Prajā-pati to them, "What would ye, that ye have stayed?"

And they said, "The Self, free from evil, ageless, deathless, sorrowless, hungerless, thirstless, real of desire, real of purpose, this should men inquire after, yea, should seek to know All worlds he wins and all desires who traces out and understands this Self This they report to be thy saying, sir, in desire thereof have we stayed"

Then Prajā-pati said to them, "The Being[2] who is seen in the eye is the Self"—thus he spake—"this is the deathless, the fearless, this is Brahma"

"Then who is he, sir, that is discerned in water and in a mirror?"

"It is he that is discerned in all these beings"

"Look upon yourselves in a basin of water," said he, "and tell me what of yourselves you do not perceive"

They looked in a basin of water, and Prajā-pati said to them, "What see you?"

"We see in this image the whole of our selves, sir," said they, "even to our hair and nails"

Then Prajā-pati said to them, "Put on goodly

[1] See above, p 85

[2] *Purusha*, cf extract i, p 56 This answer of Prajā-pati conveys the *materialistic* view of the Self, viz as the visible material body Elsewhere *Purusha* regularly denotes the *soul*

ornament and fine clothing, attire yourselves, and look in the basin of water"

They put on goodly ornament and fine clothing, attired themselves, and looked in the basin of water Prajā-pati said to them, "What see you?"

They said, "Even as we stand here wearing goodly ornament and fine clothing, and attired, sir, so are we there wearing goodly ornament and fine clothing, and attired, sir"

"This is the Self," said he, "this is the deathless, the fearless, this is Brahma"

The twain travelled away content of heart Gazing after them, Prajā-pati said "They are travelling away, yet have they not found and traced out the Self They who shall follow this doctrine, be they the gods or the demons, shall be brought low"

Now Virochana came content of heart to the demons, and declared to them this doctrine "The Self[1] should be gladdened here, the Self should be tended, he that gladdens the Self here and tends the Self gains both this world and that beyond" Therefore it is that here even now men say of one who is not bountiful nor believing nor given to sacrifice, "Fie, a demon!" For this is the doctrine of the demons, and when one has died men furnish his body with food and clothing

[1] The physical self, i e the conception of the material body

and ornament, imagining that therewith they will win the world beyond

But Indra, ere he reached the gods, foresaw this peril "Even as this [Self][1] wears goodly ornament when this body wears goodly ornament, is finely clothed when it is finely clothed, and is attired when it is attired, so likewise this [Self] becomes blind when this [body] is blind, lame when it is lame, maimed when it is maimed, yea, it perishes with the perishing of this body I see no pleasure herein"

He came back, faggots in hand Prajā-pati said to him, "Maghavā, as thou didst depart content of heart with Virochana, what wouldst thou, that thou hast come back?"

And he said "Even as this [Self], sir, wears goodly ornament when this body wears goodly ornament, is finely clothed when it is finely clothed, and is attired when it is attired, so likewise this [Self] becomes blind when this [body] is blind, lame when it is lame, maimed when it is maimed, yea, it perishes with the perishing of this body I see no pleasure herein"

"Thus indeed it is, Maghavā," said he, "but I will teach thee yet more of it Stay another two-and-thirty years"

He stayed another two-and-thirty years Then he said to him "He who wanders about re-

[1] The physical self, i e, the conception of the material body

joicing in dreams,[1] is the Self"—thus he spake—"this is the deathless, the fearless, this is Brahma"

He departed content of heart But ere he reached the gods, he foresaw this peril "This [Self] indeed becomes not blind though the body be blind, nor lame though it be lame, nor is it defiled by the defilement thereof, it is not stricken by the smiting thereof, nor is it lamed with the lameness thereof, but nevertheless it is as if it were stricken, as if it were hustled, as if it were feeling unpleasantness, as if it were weeping I see no pleasure herein"

He came back, faggots in hand Prajā-pati said to him, "Maghavā, as thou didst depart content of heart, what wouldst thou, that thou hast come back?"

And he said "This [Self] indeed becomes not blind though the body be blind, nor lame though it be lame, nor is it defiled by the defilement thereof, it is not stricken by the smiting thereof, nor is it lamed with the lameness thereof, but nevertheless it is as if it were stricken, as if it were hustled, as if it were feeling unpleasantness, as if it were weeping I see no pleasure herein"

[1] The *individual* soul or Self, which in dreams is free from the physical afflictions of empiric existence, but nevertheless is still tormented by the mental concepts of these This standpoint is that of realism

"Thus indeed it is, Maghavā," said he, "but I will teach thee yet more of it Stay another two-and-thirty years"

He stayed another two-and-thirty years Then he said to him "When one sleeps utterly and in perfect peace so that he beholds no dream,[1] this is the Self"—thus he spake—"this is the deathless, the fearless, this is Brahma"

He departed content of heart But before he reached the gods, he foresaw this peril "Truly one thus[2] knows no longer himself as 'I am,' nor these creatures He has sunk into destruction I see no pleasure herein"

He came back, faggots in hand Praja-pati said to him, "Maghavā, as thou didst depart content of heart, what wouldst thou, that thou hast come back?"

And he said "Truly, sir, one thus knows no longer himself as 'I am,' nor these creatures He has sunk into destruction I see no pleasure herein"

"Thus indeed it is, Maghavā," said he, "but I will teach thee yet more of it, it is nowhere but in this Stay another five years"

He stayed another five years These amount to one hundred and one years, so men say, "Verily Maghavā stayed for one hundred and

[1] The standpoint of pure transcendental idealism
[2] In dreamless sleep

one years as Brahman-student with Prajā-pati" Then he said to him "Verily, Maghavā, this body is mortal, held in the grasp of Death, but it is the seat of this deathless, bodiless self[1] The Embodied is held in the grasp of joy and sorrow, for what is embodied cannot be quit of joy and sorrow But joy and sorrow touch not what is unembodied Unembodied is the wind, unembodied are the cloud, the lightning, the thunder As these, rising up from yonder ether, pass into the Supreme Light and issue forth each in its own semblance, so likewise this perfect Peace, rising up from this body, passes into the Supreme Light and issues forth in its own semblance This is the Highest Spirit

Now when the eye is fixed upon the ether,

[1] Prajā-pati, in answer to Indra's criticism of his last definition of the Self, explains that the utter unconsciousness of dreamless sleep is not a state of non-being, but a state of transcendental Being-Consciousness Finite consciousness is active in embodied existence, which is attended by sensations of pleasure and pain But the finite consciousness of embodied being is but an illusive phase of the infinite consciousness of unembodied existence, which is represented by the state of dreamless sleep The great forces of cosmic nature are in essence incorporeal, when confined within the category of space or ether they produce in the macrocosm the phenomena of a finite universe, but essentially they transcend space, being the infinite powers of Absolute Being Similarly in the microcosm the physical functions which cause the conceptions of individual existence as subject of empiric thought are really phases of the Absolute Consciousness, the objectless Subject, essentially transcending individual existence

that is the spirit in the eye [which sees], the eye is but a means to see When one thinks that he will smell a thing, it is the Self, the nostril is but a means to smell When one thinks that he will utter a word, it is the Self, speech is but a means to utterance When one thinks that he will hear a thing, it is the Self, the ear is but a means to hearing When one thinks that he will think of a thing, it is the Self, the mind is his divine eye, with this divine eye he sees these desires and rejoices therein All worlds he wins and all desires who traces out and understands the Self" Thus spake Prajā-pati

XV Gloria in Excelsis [1]

I know that great Spirit, sun-hued, beyond the darkness Knowing Him, man escapeth Death, there is no other way to walk

Than this naught else is higher, nor subtler,

[1] Śvetāśvatara Upanishad, iii 8—iv 20 This work, one of the earliest metrical Upanishads, is marked by a singular combination of philosophical idealism with theistic feeling In it Brahma appears as a living God, especially in his manifestation as Śiva, or Rudra, the spirit of cosmic destruction Here accordingly we find the first expression of the doctrine of Divine Grace and of worship in love, which later became one of the chief features in Hindu religion, especially in the Vishṇuite church

nor mightier As a tree firm-set in the heavens[1] stands the One, with this Spirit the universe is filled

Formless, sorrowless is the Highest, they become deathless who know it, but others come to very grief

With face, head, neck everywhere, dwelling in covert in every creature, pervading all, the Lord is He, thus everywhere is the presence of the Gracious[2]

A great lord is the Spirit, mover of the understanding, ruler of this pure approach, Light,[3] unfading

The Spirit dwells ever as inward soul, an inch in stature, within men's hearts, conceived by the heart, the imagination, the thought, deathless they become who know this

Showing himself in the qualities of all senses, void of all senses, He is lord, ruler of all, refuge of all

Bodied in the nine-gated city,[4] the Swan hovers without, master of all the motionless and moving world[5]

Handless and footless, He speeds and seizes,

[1] Compare Kaṭh Upan vi 1 The universe is compared to an *aśvattha* tree, the *Ficus religiosa*, of which the branches are the phenomenal world and the root Brahma

[2] *Śiva*, a title of Rudra which has gradually ousted the latter name

[3] See extract vii, p 68 [4] Compare above, p 61

[5] Compare extract vii, above

eyeless, He sees , earless, He hears He knows what may be known, but there is none to know Him Men call Him the Primal, the Great Spirit

Subtler than the subtle is He, greater than the great, the soul lodged in covert in living beings Freed from grief, man sees by the Almighty's grace Him the desireless, Him the Power sovereign

I know Him, the ageless, ancient, All-soul, dwelling everywhere in universal presence, to whom Brahma-teachers deny birth, whom they call the Eternal

The one hue that by blending of powers lends manifold hues in diverse wise from gathered substance, the Beginning and End wherein the All dissolves—He is God , may He unite us with blessed understanding !

That same is the Fire, that is the Sun, that the Wind, that the Moon , that same is the Bright, that Brahma, that the Waters, that the Creator

Thou art woman, Thou art man, Thou art boy and maiden , Thou art the old man tottering on the staff , Thou art born with face looking all ways

Thou art the black bird, the green with red eyes, the lightning-bearing [cloud], the seasons, the seas , Thou art that which is beginningless, Thou livest in universal presence, whence are born all beings .

In vision of the Lord, the bounteous worshipful

God, who stands sole warder over every womb, in whom this All falls together and dissolves asunder, man comes to this everlasting peace

May He who is the fount and origin of the gods, the lord of all, Rudra, the great sage, who beheld the Germ of Gold[1] coming into being, unite us with blessed understanding

Where there is not darkness, nor day and night, nor being or not-being, but the Gracious One alone, that is the Unfading, that is the lovely [light] of Savitā[2], thence has streamed forth the ancient Intelligence

He may not be grasped above, nor athwart, nor in the midst There is no likeness of Him whose name is Great Glory

His form is not to be beheld, none sees Him with the eye Deathless they become who in heart and mind know Him as heart-dwelling

XVI THE ADVAITA-MAKARANDA OF LAKSHMĪDHARA[3]

1 Homage to Krishna of infinite bliss, the incarnate blessing of the world, who by the sun-

[1] See above, § 4

[2] The light of the sun, Ṛig-veda, III lxii 10.

[3] This is a somewhat modern poem, which is here added as it conveys with great clearness the leading psychological doctrines of the later Vedānta

beams of his glances evaporates the ocean of delusion!

2 Always I[1] am, I give light, never am I unbeloved, thus I am proved to be Brahma, consisting in Being, Thought, and Bliss

3 In me, the sky of Thought, arises the mirage of the universe[2], then how can I be aught but Brahma, knowing all, cause of all?

4 Destruction cannot come upon me from myself, because of my recognition, nor from anything else, for I have no parts, nor from the destruction of an [external] basis, for I have no such basis[3]

5 I, the ether of Thought, cannot be dried, burned, soaked, or cut even by real wind, fire, water, or weapons, much less by imaginary ones[4]

6 The universe, having no light of its own,

[1] Throughout this little work the pronoun "I" is used to denote the individual soul as witness of the sense of personality (*aham-kāra*, egoity), and the other "determinations" of soul, while itself it consciously transcends them The verse means that as the same predicates—existence, thought, and agreeableness—apply both to the soul and to Brahma, these two are identical

[2] See above, § 16

[3] The soul is eternal, for it cannot be destroyed from within, since it has self-recognition, i e continuous consciousness of self-identity, and it cannot be destroyed from without, for as it has no parts it cannot be dissolved into its parts, and as it is dependent upon nothing but itself it cannot suffer from the destruction of its basis

[4] The physical elements, which seem real, are in truth imaginary

could not possibly come to light but for the presence of light, I am the Light, and therefore am everywhere [1]

7 Without manifestation there can be no Being, without consciousness there can be no manifestation of the unconscious, and without transference there can be no union with consciousness Thus I have none beside me [2]

8 I am not body, nor organ of sense, nor vital function, nor mind, nor intelligence, for they are embraced by the idea of "mine" and are a playground for the conception of "this" [3]

9 I am the Witness, related to all things, most

[1] In the process of cognition, according to the Vedānta, there are two elements—viz the object or matter of the cognition and the subject of it The former, being wholly lifeless and inert, can only emerge into consciousness when the light of subject Thought falls upon it from without The first word of this verse, *abhā-rūpasya*, is wrongly printed *ābhā-rūpasya* and accordingly mistranslated in the "Pandit" of 1873, pp 11, 130

[2] No object exists unless it becomes cognised—i e it becomes the object of a subject conscious thereof Thus conscious being enters into relation with unconscious being, and how is this possible? It can only be explained by assuming an *adhyāsa* or "transference," an inveterate error of the individual consciousness making it identify itself with the phenomenal world, which is properly nothing more than an unreal emanation of the consciousness Hence there exists in reality nothing but consciousness See Śankara on Brahma-sūtra, i 1

[3] The sense-organs (*indriya*), vital functions (*prāna*), sensorium (*manas*), and intelligence (*dhī*, i e *buddhi*), are only "determinants," *upādhis*, external to the soul, see p 28 f

dear, I am never the Ego, for that is plunged in affections, limitations, and pains [1]

10 When the Ego is [dreamlessly] slumbering, sorrow, guilt, and activity do not appear, thus it is he who wanders, not I, who am the wanderer's witness [2]

11 The sleeper [3] knows not his sleeping, in him who sleeps not there is no dreaming and no waking I am the Witness of waking, dreaming, and dreamless sleep, and thus am not under these conditions

12 [Dreamless] sleep is a halting of [finite] understanding, dreaming and waking are the rise thereof, how can these three exist in me, who am the Witness of them and infinite of knowledge?

[1] The "witness" is the consciousness impassively cognising the affections of the psychical *upādhis*, such as love or hate It is "related to all things," for things exist only in so far as they are objects of thought (see v 7) It is thus universal Being, Thought, and Bliss On the error of confusing the absolute Self with the Ego, see p 45 The Ego (*aham-kāra*) is really the subject of dreaming and dreamless sleep and waking, not the transcendental Self, according to the later Vedānta

[2] In deep sleep or swoons the Ego or sense of personality disappears and with it disappear its resultant activities and affections, hence the *samsāra*, or continuance of rebirth, which consists essentially of these activities, cannot co-exist with the absence of the Ego, i e with the condition of abstract impersonal self-consciousness

[3] The Ego, or sense of personality, which in dreamless sleep is unconscious that it is sleeping On the other hand the transcendental Soul or Self is everlastingly conscious, it is the "Witness" of the three states

13 I am the one who knows the beings of six-fold change,[1] and myself changeless, were it not so, I should be altogether incapable of observing their changes

14 For a changing thing goes again and again through birth and dissolution in this and that form, how can it be an observer of these [changes]?

15 Nor can any one behold his own birth and destruction, for these are [respectively] the last and first moments of antecedent and subsequent non-being[2]

16 How can the not-Light touch the Self which is Light itself, and by whose light alone are caused the words, "I give not light"?[3]

17 Nevertheless there is apparent in the sky

[1] The six changes of finite being are origin, continuance, increase, attainment of maturity, commencement of decay, and dissolution As subject of the cognition of these phenomena, the Soul must be itself devoid of these properties

[2] If the Soul were liable to changes, it would be conscious of its changes, which is not the case (verse 14) Every change of a thing implies destruction of its previous condition, hence, even if we could imagine soul as passing through the six changes, we should have to admit that when it is in a particular state it cannot as such be conscious of itself at the beginning of that state (which is the last moment of the previous state), nor can it be conscious of itself at the end of that state (which is the first moment of the next state)

[3] The illusion of a phenomenal world cannot be in any real connection with the pure consciousness of the absolute Soul, for the conception of a physical world opposed to thought is essentially a partial negation of consciousness by consciousness, and nothing more

of Thought a certain mist which subsists on the lack of reflection and ends with the rise of the sun of reflection [1]

18 In this long-drawn dream of which our world is made, and which arises from the great slumber of Self-ignorance, there appear Heaven, Salvation, and the other phantoms [2]

19 This distinction between unconscious and conscious being is imaginarily imposed on me, the conscious being, like the distinction between moving and motionless figures in a picture on a level wall

20 Even my Witnesshood is unreal, is but a colouring reflected from the objects of thought, it merely suggests the billowless ocean of Thought [3]

21 I, the ocean of ambrosia, decay not because phantom bubbles arise, I, the mountain of crystal, am not flushed by the play of dream-fashioned evening clouds [4]

[1] The illusion of the phenomenal world, which falsely appears as really existent, until its unreality is proved by "reflection"

[2] Even salvation, or release of the Soul (*moksha*), is only real from the standpoint of empiric thought The transcendent Self is never in bondage, and therefore is never released

[3] Since the objects of finite Thought are strictly unreal, there cannot be a *real* consciousness of them in the real Self The function of witness of phenomena which apparently is exercised by the Self is really a mere indication of the absolute supra-phenomenal immobility of consciousness which is characteristic of the real Self

[4] The essential nature of the Soul is in no way affected by

22 *Being* is my very essence, not a property, like ether's being, for as there is no Being save me, no class-concept [of Being] can be allowed [1]

23 *Knowledge* is my very essence, not a quality, if it were a quality, [Soul] would be if intelligible not-Self, and if unintelligible non-being [2]

24 *Bliss* am I, which is naught else [but me], were it aught else, it would not be bliss, for if not subordinate to me, it would not be agreeable, and if subordinate, it could not be of itself agreeable

25 No real thing forsooth can ever be of diverse essences, thus I am without inward distinction, void of the differences arising from the world

26 By the words "That art thou" is indicated a Power of single essence, pure by the absence of the variety [consisting in] the transcendence [of

the emergence from it of an imaginary universe, nor by the false idea, reflected upon it from the illusory universe without, that it is a subject or object of action, etc

1 We must not say that "existence" is only a property or attribute of the Soul For an attribute is a generic concept implying more than one individual in which it resides, but in the case of Soul there is only one individual, the Soul itself, in which resides the attribute "existence," in the same way as in the phenomenal world there is only one ether, or space, in which therefore "etherhood" is essence, not attribute

2 If the Self is an object to its assumed property of knowledge, it is no longer Self, for the object of knowledge cannot be identical with the subject (which here is the property of knowledge) If again the Self is not an object of its knowledge, the Self is non-existent, for the incogitable is unreal

the Supreme] and the distinction [of individual souls] [1]

27 I am the Power self-authoritative and absolute, in which are stilled the phantom figures of the world and separate souls, of disciples and masters

28 May this "Nectar of Monism" of the poet Lakshmīdhara, gathered from the autumnal lotuses of poesy, be drunk by the scholar-bees.

[1] See Appendix I

APPENDIX I

THE SAMBANDHAS

The 25th and 26th verses of the Advaita-makaranda given above refer to a topic of importance in the later Vedānta, viz the logical relation (*sambandha*) of terms The relations are three (1) "common reference," *sāmānādhikaranya*, (2) "relation as predicate (*viśeshana*) and subject (*viśeshya*)," and (3) "relation as indicated (*lakshya*) and indicative term (*lakshanā*)" The proposition "Thou art That," *tat tvam asi*, which is the key-note of the Vedānta (see p 24), comes under all these categories The term *That* denotes literally the whole aggregate of Ignorances together with the omniscient cosmic consciousness "determined" by the latter and with the transcendental consciousness (see p 30), but by "indication" or metonymy (*lakshanā*) it signifies only the transcendental consciousness The term *Thou* literally denotes the aggregate of Ignorances conceived distributively (see p 30 f) together with limited individual consciousness "determined" by the latter, and with unlimited consciousness , and by "indication" it signifies only the last Now the proposition *Thou art That* comes under the relation of "common reference", for both *Thou* and *That* signify *Consciousness* (Brahma), in the former case as transcending perception, in the latter case as manifested to perception in the form of finite distinction Again, these terms are related as subject and predicate, that is, they are identified in thought by abstraction of their difference (their difference lying in the fact that the one transcends perception, and the other does not) Lastly, these terms have a metonymic relation When we have abstracted the difference already mentioned, we may use both to signify the Consciousness, *That* being the "indicated" and *Thou* the "indicative" term In the same way the three several terms *Being*, *Thought*, and *Bliss*, after due abstraction of difference (namely phenomenal distinctions) designate "indicatively" the single indivisible Brahma essentially characterised by infinite being, thought, and bliss For further details of the Hindu theories on these subjects see Vedānta-sāra, Jacob's translation, p 83 f , Athalye's notes on Tarka-sangraha, § 59, Kāvya-prakāśa, ch ii , etc

APPENDIX II

LIST OF THE CHIEF UPANISHADS

The following list gives the names of the most ancient and important Upanishads, together with the contractions used for them in the preceding pages The canon generally accepted in modern India contains 108 Upanishads, most of these are however comparatively late and distinctly sectarian (later Vedāntī, Vishnuite, Śivaite, Yogī, Sannyāsī, etc)

B A	Brihad-āranyaka	Upanishad
Ch	Chhāṇdogya	,,
Taitt	Taittirīya	,,
Ait	Aitareya	,,
Kau	Kaushītaki	,,
Kena	Kena (Talavakāra)	,,
Kath	Katha	,,
Īśa	Īśāvāsya	,,
Śvet	Svetāśvatara	,,
Mund	Mundaka	,,
	Mahā-nārāyana	,,
Pra	Praśna	,,
Maitr	Maitrāyanīya	,,
Mānd	Māndūkya	,,

BIBLIOGRAPHY

The beginner will find the following works useful

SACRED BOOKS OF THE EAST, edited by F Max Muller vol 1 & 15, Upanishads, translated by F Max Muller, vol 34, Vedānta-sūtra (i e Brahma-sūtra) with the commentary by Śankara, translated by G Thibaut *Oxford, Clarendon Press*, 1879, etc

PHILOSOPHY OF THE UPANISHADS, by A E Gough *London, Trubner*, 1882

THE UPANISHADS (in Sanskrit and English) and Śankara's commentary (in English), translated by Sītārāma Śāstri and Gangānātha Jhā *Madras, Seshachari*, 1898, etc

SECHZIG UPANISHADS DES VEDA, ubersetzt von Dr Paul Deussen *Leipzig, Brockhaus*, 1897

THE PHILOSOPHY OF THE UPANISHADS, by Paul Deussen Translated by Rev A Geden *Edinburgh, T & T Clark*, 1906

DAS SYSTEM DES VEDANTA, von P Deussen *Leipzig, Brockhaus*, 1883

THE SIX SYSTEMS OF INDIAN PHILOSOPHY, by F Max Muller *London, Longmans*, 1899

Of the numerous compendia of the later Vedānta we may mention two which have been published in English—the Vedānta-sāra of Sadānanda, translated under the title "A Manual of Hindu Pantheism" by Col G A Jacob (*London, Trubner*, 1881), and the Advaita-makaranda of Lakshmīdhara, with Svayamprakāśa's commentary, translated by A E Gough in "The Pandit," vol 8, 9 (*Benares*, 1873)

Of the chief *Sanskrit* texts of the Vedānta schools numerous editions have been published in India Among the best are those issued in the "Anandāśrama Sanskrit Series" from the Ānandāśrama Press, Poona

The student is not likely to derive much exact knowledge from the publications of irresponsible neo-vedantic societies in Europe and America These bodies have the commendable object of making the principles of the Vedānta intelligible to modern Western thinkers , but until they display a more scientific and historical spirit their success is likely to be limited

Printed by Hazell, Watson & Viney, Ld , London and Aylesbury

THE ORIENT LIBRARY

THE

WISDOM OF THE EAST SERIES

Edited by L CRANMER-BYNG and Dr S A KAPADIA

THE object of the Editors of this Series is a very definite one They desire above all things that, in their humble way, these books shall be the ambassadors of good will and understanding between East and West, the old world of Thought and the new of Action In this endeavour, and in their own sphere, they are but followers of the highest example in the land They are confident that a deeper knowledge of the great ideals and lofty philosophy of Oriental thought may help to a revival of that true spirit of Charity which neither despises nor fears the nations of another creed and colour Finally, in thanking press and public for the very cordial reception given to the "Wisdom of the East" Series, they wish to state that no pains have been spared to secure the best specialists for the treatment of the various subjects at hand

---

LONDON

JOHN MURRAY, ALBEMARLE STREET, W.

(Please order through your Bookseller)

WISDOM OF THE EAST SERIES

Brahma-Knowledge: An Outline of the Philosophy of the Vedānta

As set forth by the Upanishads and by Śankara By L D BARNETT, M A , LITT D , Professor of Sanskrit at University College, London 2/- net

The Sayings of Confucius

A new Translation of the greater part of the Confucian Analects with Introduction and Notes by LIONEL GILES, M A (Oxon), Assistant in the Department of Oriental Books and Manuscripts of the British Museum 2/ net

Arabian Wisdom

Selections and Translations from the Arabic by JOHN WORTABET, M D 1/- net

The Persian Mystics

Jalálu'd-dín Rúmí

By F HADLAND DAVIS 2/- net

The Way of the Buddha

Selections from the Buddhist texts, together with the original Pali, with Introduction by HERBERT BAYNES, M R A S 2/ net

Sadi's Scroll of Wisdom

By SHAIKH SA'DI With Introduction by ARTHUR N WOLLASTON, C I E 1/ net

Musings of a Chinese Mystic

Selections from the Philosophy of Chuang Tzŭ With Introduction by LIONEL GILES, M A (Oxon), Assistant at the British Museum 2/- net

The Instruction of Ptah-Hotep and the Instruction of Ke'gemni

The Oldest Books in the World Translated from the Egyptian with Introduction and Appendix by BATTISCOMBE G GUNN 1/- net

The Wisdom of Israel Being Extracts from the Babylonian Talmud and Midrash Rabboth

Translated from the Aramaic with an Introduction by EDWIN COLLINS 1/- net

WISDOM OF THE EAST SERIES

The Rose Garden of Sa'di

Selected and Rendered from the Persian with Introduction by L CRANMER-BYNG 1/- net

Women and Wisdom of Japan

With Introduction by S TAKAISHI 1/- net.

The Classics of Confucius

I The Book of History (Shu-King)

By W GORN OLD 1/- net

II The Book of Odes (Shi-King)

By L CRANMER-BYNG 1/- net

The Awakening of the Soul

From the Arabic of IBN TUFAIL Translated with Introduction by PAUL BRÖNNLE, Ph D 1/6 net

The Religion of the Koran

With Introduction by ARTHUR N WOLLASTON, C I E 1/ net

The Sayings of Lao Tzŭ

From the Chinese Translated with Introduction by LIONEL GILES, of the British Museum 1/ net

The Duties of the Heart

By RABBI BACHYE Translated from the Hebrew with Introduction by EDWIN COLLINS, Hollier Hebrew Scholar, U C L 1/- net

The Teachings of Zoroaster and the Philosophy of the Parsi Religion

Translated with Introduction by DR S A KAPADIA, Lecturer University College, London 2/- net

---

All literary communications to be addressed to the Editors of

THE ORIENT LIBRARY, c/o DR S A KAPADIA, ORIENTAL SECRETARY, NORTHBROOK SOCIETY, 185 PICCADILLY, LONDON, W

EXTRACTS FROM A FEW PRESS OPINIONS

The Athenæum —"We wish that there were more of them, they are dreamy, lifelike, and fascinating"

St James's Gazette —"The quaint and picturesque little 'Wisdom of the East' Series"

Pall Mall Gazette —"No translation of this important work has been made since the beginning of the eighteenth century"

The Academy —"Slim, tastefully bound little volumes"

Manchester Courier —"Worthy of close study by all who would penetrate to the depth of Eastern thought and feeling"

Literary Guide —"We wish success to this little series of books"

Outlook —"This Series is published to help in the process of renewing the spiritual and moral life of the West"

The Scotsman —"This Series should not fail to please readers of the more studious sort"

Nottingham Press —"This dainty little Volume is the fifth of the Series, all the Earlier Volumes of which have been cordially welcomed by Press and Public alike"

Southport Guardian —"This Series will find considerable favour with all Students of Eastern Literature and Eastern Philosophy"

The Northern Weekly —"I must confess that I am attracted by the Literature of the East This week I have been reading the dainty little books issued by the Orient Press"

Bristol Mercury —"We commend these little books to all who imagine that there is no knowledge worth having outside Europe and America"

Glasgow Herald.—"This new Series has a definite and lofty aim, and is deserving of support The books are small, cheap, and well adapted for the pocket Every page is regularly refreshing and stimulating"

North Devon Journal.—"The difference between Eastern and Western modes of thought is pointedly exemplified by this Series

Halifax Guardian —"They are well worth perusal and are presented to the reader in that attractive form which the Orient Press has been happy enough to hit on"

Jewish Chronicle —"No such near approach to an English translation has ever been made"

Christian Age —"Meditation on the teaching of this little book cannot but be helpful to all its readers"

Field —"Such books are valuable aids to the understanding of a far-off age and people, and have a great interest for the student of literature"

Irish Times —"The volumes are charming in form, low in price, and excellent in matter"

Publishers' Circular —"We unhesitatingly recommend them to all who can appreciate the ideal of goodness and holiness and the highest form of culture"

Public Opinion —"These tiny books have much to commend them"

LONDON JOHN MURRAY, ALBEMARLE STREET, W.

(Please order through your Bookseller)

Elphinstone, Hon M HISTORY OF INDIA—the Hindú and Mahometan Periods With Notes and additions by E B COWELL, M A. *Ninth Edition* Demy 8vo 15*s* net

Fanshawe, H C DELHI PAST AND PRESENT With Maps and Illustrations *Cheap Edition* Demy 8vo 8*s* net

Handbook INDIA, BURMA AND CEYLON, including Bengal, Bombay and Madras, the Panjab, North-West Provinces, Rajputana, the Central Provinces, Mysore, etc, the Native States and Assam With 78 Maps and Plans of Towns and Buildings *Sixth Edition* Crown 8vo 20*s*

Indian Records Series. Published for the Government of India —

BENGAL IN 1756–57 A Selection of Public and Private Papers dealing with the Affairs of the British in Bengal during the reign of Siraj-Uddaula Edited, with Notes and an Historical Introduction, by S C HILL, B A, B Sc 3 Vols Medium 8vo 12*s* net each Vol

OLD FORT WILLIAM IN BENGAL A Selection of Official Documents dealing with its History Edited by C R WILSON, M A, D Litt 2 Vols Medium 8vo 12*s* net each Vol

Indian Text Series Edited by T W RHYS DAVIDS, Ph D, LL D

STORIA DO MOGOR, OR, THE MOGUL MEMOIRS (1653—1708) By NICCOLAO MANUCCI, Venetian Translated and edited, with Notes and Introduction, under the supervision of the Royal Asiatic Society, by WILLIAM IRVINE Medium 8vo 4 Vols 12*s*. net each Vol

Crooke, William THINGS INDIAN Being Discursive Notes on various subjects connected with India Demy 8vo. 12*s* net

Eggar, Mrs H C AN INDIAN GARDEN With Coloured Frontispiece and 18 Illustrations Square Demy 8vo 7*s* 6*d* net

Lyall, Sir Alfred ASIATIC STUDIES, Religious and Social 2 Vols *Cheaper Edition* Demy 8vo 5*s* net each

—— THE RISE AND EXPANSION OF THE BRITISH DOMINION IN INDIA *Cheap Edition* With 5 Maps Demy 8vo 5*s* each

Murray, A H Hallam THE HIGH ROAD OF EMPIRE Reproductions in Colour of 47 Water-Colour Drawings and numerous Pen and Ink Sketches made in India. Medium 8vo 21*s* net Edition de Luxe, £2 2*s* net

Yule, Colonel Sir Henry THE BOOK OF SER MARCO POLO, the Venetian, concerning the Kingdoms and Marvels of the East Sir Henry Yule's Translation, revised throughout in the light of Modern Discoveries by Professor HENRI CORDIER With a Memoir of Henry Yule, by his DAUGHTER With Maps and Illustrations 2 Vols Medium 8vo £3 3*s* net

—— and **Burnell**, Arthur Coke HOBSON-JOBSON Being a Glossary of Anglo-Indian Colloquial Words and Phrases and of Kindred Terms, Etymological, Historical, Geographical and Discursive *New Edition* Thoroughly revised by WILLIAM CROOKE Demy 8vo 28*s* net

Yusuf-Ali, A LIFE AND LABOUR IN INDIA With Illustrations Including Drawings by Native Artists Demy 8vo 12*s* net

---

JOHN MURRAY, ALBEMARLE STREET, W

Published by

Facsimile Publisher
Ashok Vihar, Delhi-110052 (India)
Website: www.facsimilepublisher.com

Distributed by

Gyan Books Pvt. Ltd.
5, Ansari Road, Daryaganj, New Delhi-110002 (India)
E-mail: books@gyanbooks.com, Website: www.gyanbooks.com